YOUTH EDITION

HENRY T. BLACKABY & CLAUDE V. KING

Experiencing God

KNOWING AND DOING THE WILL OF GOD

LIFEWAY PRESS
NASHVILLE, TENNESSEE

LifeWay Press books are published by The Sunday School Board
127 Ninth Avenue, North, Nashville, Tennessee 37234

Dewey Decimal Number: 231.5
Subject Heading: GOD–WILL

This book has been adapted for youth from the original adult edition
of *Experiencing God: Knowing and Doing the Will of God.* With the exception of Units 1 and 3,
new unit introductions were written specifically for youth.

Experiencing God, Youth Edition is the text for course number CG-0085 in the subject area "Ministry" of the
Christian Growth Study Plan.

We believe the Bible has God for its author, salvation for its end, and truth
without any mixture of error, for its matter. The 1963 statement
of *The Baptist Faith and Message* is our doctrinal guideline.

Printed in the United States of America
Available from Baptist Book Stores and LifeWay Christian Stores

Youth Section
Discipleship and Family Development Division
The Sunday School Board of the Southern Baptist Convention
127 Ninth Avenue, North,
Nashville, Tennessee 37234

CONTENTS

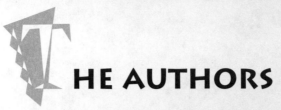

THE AUTHORS

HENRY T. BLACKABY is Director of the Office of Prayer and Spiritual Awakening at the Home Mission Board of the Southern Baptist Convention. A graduate of the University of British Columbia, Vancouver, Canada, and Golden Gate Baptist Theological Seminary, he pastored a church in the Los Angeles area after seminary. Then he accepted a call to Faith Baptist Church in Saskatoon, Saskatchewan. He authored a book entitled *What the Spirit Is Saying to the Churches* in which he recounts the moving activity of God in the midst of His people at Faith Baptist Church. During Henry's 12 years in Saskatoon this church helped to start 38 new churches and missions of the new churches.

Before coming to the Home Mission Board, Henry served as Director of Missions in Vancouver, British Columbia. He has written for numerous publications and serves on the Bold Mission PRAYER Thrust committee of the Southern Baptist Convention. He has led conferences throughout the United States, Canada, and in Zambia and Austria. He provides leadership for the development of prayer and spiritual awakening in the life of the Southern Baptist Convention in conjunction with SBC agencies and state, associational, and local church leadership.

His wife is the former Marilynn Sue Wells. They have five children: Richard, Thomas, Melvin, Norman, and Carrie. All five children have responded to God's call to church-related ministry or missions.

CLAUDE V. KING is Mission Service Corps Consultant, Office of Prayer and Spiritual Awakening, Home Mission Board of the Southern Baptist Convention. He is active in discipleship training and is becoming recognized as a writer of interactive learning activities. Claude coauthored another LIFE course with John Drakeford entitled *WiseCounsel: Skills for Lay Counseling.* He has served as a volunteer church planter for the Concord Baptist Association of middle Tennessee. A native of Tennessee, he is a graduate of Belmont College and New Orleans Baptist Theological Seminary. He lives in Murfreesboro, Tennessee, with his wife, Reta, and daughters, Julie and Jenny.

BRENT GAMBRELL is a member of Images Creative Group, a drama team that travels the nation communicating the Word of God and precepts of Christ by utilizing contemporary situations to portray biblical principles. On many occasions, he has been a faculty member, as well as an entertainment feature, for youth discipleship retreats. For several years Brent served as Events Coordinator at Two Rivers Baptist Church, Nashville, Tennessee.

Editor's Note. In the following materials Henry Blackaby is the primary author of content materials. As your personal tutor, he will speak to you just as if he were sitting at your side as you study. Claude King has written the learning activities to assist you in your study. Brent Gambrell has written the unit introductions for Units 2 and 4-9.

The personal illustrations of the authors are written solely from their personal viewpoints. Others who were involved, if given the opportunity, could write a different and more complete account. The point of agreement, however, would center on God's activity as He accomplished things that only can be explained in terms of His divine presence and activity.

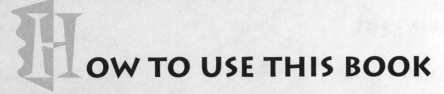

HOW TO USE THIS BOOK

Right away you will notice that this book is different from most books you read. It is not designed for you to sit down and read from cover to cover. It is designed for you to carefully study, understand, and apply biblical principles to your life. It is about experiencing God, day-by-day, moment-by-moment.

To get the most out of this course, you must take your time by studying only one day's lesson at a time. Do not try to study through several lessons in one day. You need time to let the new information and ideas "sink in." You are wanting to experience a Person—Jesus Christ. Time and meditation are necessary to allow the Holy Spirit to make Christ real in your life.

The learning activities will begin (like this paragraph) with a symbol pointing you to indented type. Follow the instructions given to complete the activity. After you have completed the activity you will continue reading.

Normally, you will be given answers following the activity, so you can check your work. Write your own answer before reading mine. Sometimes your response to the activity will be your personal response or opinion, and no right or wrong answer can be given. If you have difficulty with an activity, write a note in the margin. Discuss the answer with your leader or small group.

Do not skip any of the learning activities. Each one is designed to help you learn and apply to life the truths presented in the content. If you leave out any of these activities, you may miss an encounter with God that could change your life.

Do not skip any of the learning activities.

At the end of each day's lesson, I will ask you to review the lesson and pray. As you review and pray, do the following:

Review

Pray

• Ask God to identify for you one or more statements or Scriptures from the lesson that He wants you to understand, learn, or practice. This is a personal application question that has no wrong answer. If God causes a statement or Scripture to be meaningful to you, that is the correct response.
• Reword the statement or Scripture you select into a prayer of response. Pray about what God may want you to do in response to the truths learned.
• You may want to take notes in the margin each day as you study. God may reveal several responses He wants you to make to a particular lesson. Don't let those thoughts get away from you. Write them down so you can review them. You may even want to keep a notebook for recording your spiritual journey. *DiscipleHelps: A Daily Quiet Time Guide and Journal* would be helpful for recording thoughts and ideas. I will talk to you more about a journal later on.

Take Notes

Once each week you should attend a small-group session that is designed to help you discuss the ideas and concepts you studied the previous week, share insights and testimonies, encourage one another, and pray together. An attractive diploma from the Church Study Course system is awarded for those who complete a course like this in a small-group study (see p. 160 for details).

If you have started studying *Experiencing God, Youth Edition*, and you are not involved in a small group, enlist a few friends to study through the course with you. You will discover that other members of the body of Christ can help you more fully know and understand God's will.

Small-group Study

I am praying that God will use this course to radically touch your life for the Kingdom's sake. His work in your life will far surpass all your plans and dreams. He will bring purpose and fulfillment into your life with overflowing joy.

GOD'S WILL AND YOUR LIFE

Unit

1

THE WORLD'S FAIR

In 1986, when the World's Fair was coming to Vancouver, our association of churches was convinced God wanted us to try to reach the 22 million people that would come to the fair. We had about two thousand members in our churches in the greater Vancouver area. How in the world could two thousand people make a great impact on such a mass of tourists from all over the world? Both youth and adults had some exciting ideas.

Two years before the fair we began to set our plans in motion. At that time, the total income for our whole association was $9 thousand. The following year our income was about $16 thousand. For the year of the World's Fair we took a great leap of faith and set a budget for $202 thousand. We had commitments that would probably provide 35 percent of that budget. Sixty-five percent of the budget was dependent on prayer.

Can you operate a budget on prayer? Yes. But when you do that, you are attempting something only God can do. What do most of us do? We set the practical budget, which is the total of what we can do. Then we set a hope or faith budget. The budget we generally trust and use, however, is the one we can reach by ourselves. We do not really trust God to do anything.

As an association of churches, we decided that God had definitely led us to the work that would cost $202 thousand. That became our operating budget. All of our people began praying for God to provide and to guide us in doing everything we believed He wanted us to do during the World's Fair.

At the end of the year, I asked our treasurer how much money we had received. From Canada, the United States, and other parts of the world we had received $264 thousand. But people did more than give money. They came from all over the world to assist us. During the course of the fair, we became a catalyst to see almost 20 thousand people come to know Jesus Christ as Lord and Savior. God had truly moved—far beyond anyone's expectations!

We cannot explain what happened at the World's Fair except in terms of God's intervention. Only God could have accomplished those results. And how did God do it? He did it with believers of all ages who had determined to be servants, who were moldable, flexible, and available for the Master's use.

Verse to Memorize
This Week

I am the vine; you are the branches. If a man remains in me and I in him, he will bear much fruit; apart from me you can do nothing.

–JOHN 15:5

JESUS IS YOUR WAY

Jesus said, "This is eternal life: that they may know you, the only true God, and Jesus Christ, whom you have sent" (John 17:3). The heart of eternal life and the heart of this study is for you to KNOW GOD and to KNOW JESUS CHRIST whom He has sent.

Knowing God does not come through a program or a method. It is a relationship with a Person. It is an intimate love relationship with God. Through this relationship, God reveals His will and invites you to join Him where He is already at work. When you obey God, He accomplishes through you something only He can do.

Jesus said, "I have come that they may have life, and have it to the full" (John 10:10). Would you like to experience life to the full? You may, if you are willing to respond to God's invitation to an intimate love relationship with Him. I want to help you move into the kind of relationship with God that will enable you to experience eternal life to the fullest degree possible.

Relationship to Jesus Christ—the Beginning Point

Since you are taking this course, I assume that you have already trusted Jesus Christ as Savior, and you acknowledge Him to be Lord of your life. If you have not made this most important decision in your life, the rest of the course will have little meaning for you because spiritual matters can only be understood by those who have the indwelling Spirit of Christ (1 Cor. 2:14).

If you sense a need to accept Jesus as your Savior and Lord, now is the time to settle this matter with God. Ask God to speak to you as you read the following Scriptures:

- Romans 3:23—All have sinned.
- Romans 6:23—Eternal life is a free gift of God.
- Romans 5:8—Because of love, Jesus paid the death penalty for your sins.
- Romans 10:9-10—Confess Jesus as Lord.
- Romans 10:13—Ask God to save you, and He will.

To place your faith in Jesus and receive His gift of eternal life you must:

- Recognize that you are a sinner and that you need a saving relationship with Jesus Christ.
- Confess (agree with God about) your sins.
- Repent of your sins (turn from sin to God).
- Ask Jesus to save you by His grace.
- Turn over the rule in your life to Jesus. Let Him be your Lord.

If you need help, call your pastor, youth leader, or a Christian friend. If you have just made this important decision, call someone and share the good news of what God has done in your life. Then share your decision with your church.

Looking for More in Your Experience with God?

You may be frustrated in your Christian experience, because you know God has a more abundant life for you than you have experienced. Or you may be earnestly desiring God's directions for your life and ministry. You may have experienced

As you follow Jesus one day at a time, He will keep you right in the center of God's will.

Not a program

Not a method

A love relationship with God

"The man without the Spirit does not accept the things that come from the Spirit of God, for they are foolishness to him, and he cannot understand them, because they are spiritually discerned."
—1 Corinthians 2:14

tragedy in your life and don't know what to do. Whatever your present circumstances may be, my earnest prayer is that somehow in this time together you will be able to:

• Hear when God is speaking to you.
• Clearly identify the activity of God in your life.
• Believe God to be and do everything He promises.
• Adjust your beliefs, character, and behavior to God and His ways.
• See what God wants to do through your life.
• Clearly know what you need to do in response to God's activity in your life.
• Experience God doing through you what only God can do!

Your study guide

Reaching these goals is an impossible task for this course. These are things only God can do in your life. For your deeper walk with God, I will try to serve as your guide and encourager. I will be sharing with you some of the "wonderful works" the Lord has done as God's people have applied biblical principles to following God. In the activities I will invite you to interact with God, so He can reveal to you the ways He wants you to apply these principles in your own life.

 Read John 14:26. Fill in the blanks to tell what this verse says the Holy Spirit will do.

The Holy Spirit will _____ you _____ things.

Your Teacher

"But the Counselor, the Holy Spirit, whom the Father will send in my name, will teach you all things."

—John 14:26

The Holy Spirit of God will be your personal Teacher (John 14:26). He is the One who will guide you to apply biblical principles according to God's will. He will confirm in your heart the truth of Scripture. Therefore, your intimate relationship with God in prayer, meditation, and Bible study will be an essential part of this course. Let the Spirit of God bring you into an intimate relationship with the God of the universe "who is able to do immeasurably more than all we ask or imagine, according to his power that is at work within us" (Eph. 3:20).

Let Jesus Be Your Way

For 12 years I was pastor of a church in Saskatoon, Saskatchewan, Canada. One day a farmer said to me, "Henry, come out and visit with me at my farm." He then gave me directions that I wrote down. One day, with the directions in hand, I set out for the farm. After many wrong turns, I finally got there.

The next time I went to the farmer's house, the farmer was with me. What did I have to do to get there? I simply had to listen to him and obey him. Every time he said, "turn," I did just what he said. The farmer was my "map," because he knew the way.

 When you come to Jesus to seek His will for your life, which of the following requests is most like what you ask? Check your response.

❏ 1. Lord, what do You want me to do? When do You want me to do it? And please tell me what the outcome will be.
❏ 2. Lord, just tell me what to do one step at a time, and I will do it.

Isn't the first choice the most typical way we respond? We are always asking God for a detailed "road map." We say, "Lord, if You could just tell me where I am heading, then I will be able to set my course and go."

He says, "You don't need to. What you need to do is follow Me one day at a time." We need to come to the place where the second response is ours.

"I am the way and the truth and the life."

—John 14:6

Who is it that really knows the way for you to go to fulfill God's purpose for your life? Jesus is. He said, "I am the way."

If you were to do everything Jesus tells you one day at a time, do you suppose that you always would be right in the center of where God wants you to be? Check your response.

❏ 1. No, Jesus does not really know God's will for my life.
❏ 2. No, Jesus might mislead me and take me the wrong way.
❏ 3. Well, Jesus would rather I wait until He tells me all the details before I start to follow Him.
❏ 4. Yes, if I follow Jesus one day at a time, I will be right in the center of God's will for my life.

When you get to the place where you trust Jesus to guide you one step at a time, you will experience a new freedom. If you don't trust Jesus to guide you this way, you will worry every time you make a turn. You will often freeze up and cannot make a decision. This is not the way God intends for you to live your life.

Abram Followed One Day at a Time

Abram (later, God changed his name to Abraham) is a good example of the one-day-at-a-time principle at work in a Bible personality.

Walking by Faith

 Read about the call of Abram to do God's will. Notice how much information he was given before he was asked to follow. Underline where he was to go and what he was to do.

> The LORD had said to Abram, "Leave your country, your people and your father's household and go to the land I will show you" (Gen. 12:1).

> Abram was seventy-five years old when he set out from Haran. He took his wife Sarai, his nephew Lot, all the possessions they had accumulated and the people they had acquired in Haran, and they set out for the land of Canaan, and they arrived there (Gen. 12:4-5).

What did God say? How specific was He? "Leave" and "go." Go where? "To a land I will show you."

 Are you ready to follow God's will that way? Check your response.

❏ 1. NO, I don't think God will ever ask me to go anywhere that He doesn't show me ahead of time where I am going.
❏ 2. I'm not sure.
❏ 3. YES, I am willing to follow Him by faith and not by sight.
❏ 4. OTHER:_____

Many times, as with Abram, God called people just to follow Him. (Tomorrow you will read about several.) He is more likely to call you to follow one day at a time than He is to spell out all the details before you begin to obey Him. As we continue our study together, you will find this truth active in the lives of many biblical personalities.

Read Matthew 6:33-34 at the right; then pause and pray.

- Agree that God is absolutely trustworthy.
- Agree with God that you will follow Him one day at a time.
- Agree that you will follow God even when He does not spell out all the details.
- Agree that you will let God be your Way.

"Seek first his kingdom and his righteousness, and all these things will be given to you as well. Therefore do not worry about tomorrow, for tomorrow will worry about itself. Each day has enough trouble of its own."

—Matthew 6:33-34

If you cannot agree to these actions right now, openly confess your struggles to God. Ask Him to help you want to do His will in His way. Claim the promise: "It is God who works in you to will and to act according to his good purpose" (Phil. 2:13).

As I noted at the beginning of this book, at the end of each day's lesson, I will ask you to review the lesson and pray. Following are the review items. Today, I will suggest some possible ways you could respond to the items. After today, you are on your own.

 Review today's lesson. Pray and ask God to identify one or more statements or Scriptures that He wants you to understand, learn, or practice. Then respond to the following:

What was the most meaningful statement or Scripture you read today?

_____

Reword the statement or Scripture into a prayer of response to God.

_____

_____

What does God want you to do in response to today's study?

_____

After today's lesson a person might have responded like this:

What was the most meaningful statement or Scripture you read today?

Jesus is my way. I don't need a complete road map to stay in the center of God's will.

Reword the statement or Scripture into a prayer of response to God.

Lord I will follow You even if I don't know the way.

What does God want you to do in response to today's study?

I need to quit worrying about tomorrow and trust Jesus to guide me one day at a time.

 Write out your memory verse for this unit. You may use a different translation for your memory verses, if you prefer. Practice your memory verses daily.

SUMMARY STATEMENTS
• As I follow Jesus one day at a time, He will keep me in the center of God's will.
• Jesus is my way. I don't need any other road map.

Now, to review the suggestions for completing each lesson of this course, read again "How to Use This Book" (p. 5). Note the following points:
• Study only ONE lesson each day, Monday through Friday.
• The symbol marks each learning activity.
• Complete ALL of the learning activities. Do not skip any.
• Attend a small-group session once a week.

JESUS IS YOUR MODEL

Interpret Experience by Scripture

During this course and during your life you will have times when you want to respond based on your own experiences or your own wisdom. Such an approach will get you in trouble. This should be your guideline: Always go back to the Bible for truth (or, for the Holy Spirit to reveal truth).

> Look to see what God says and how He works in the Scriptures. Make your decisions and evaluate your experiences based on biblical principles.

When you study the Scriptures, do not base your decision on one isolated case. Look to see how God works throughout the Scriptures. When you learn how God has worked throughout history, you can depend on His working in a similar way with you. Your experience is valid only as it is confirmed in the Scriptures.

I never deny any experience that a person has had. I always reserve the right, however, to interpret it according to what I understand in the Scriptures. At times individuals get upset with me and say, "Well, I don't care what you say, I've experienced this."

I respond as kindly as I know by saying, "I do not deny your experience. I do question your interpretation of what you experienced, because it is contrary to what I see in the Word of God."

Experiences alone cannot be our guide. Every experience must be controlled and understood by the Scriptures. The God revealed in Scripture does not change.

To see if you have grasped this idea, mark the following statements as T (true) or F (false).

_____ 1. Human interpretations of my experiences are an effective way to know and follow God.

_____ 2. I should always evaluate my experiences based on the truths I find in the Word of God.

_____ 3. I may get a distorted understanding of God if I do not check my experiences against the truths of Scripture.

_____ 4. I can trust God to work in my life in ways similar to how I see Him working throughout the Scriptures.

Number 1 is false; 2, 3, and 4 are true. Number 1 is false because experiences must be interpreted in the light of the Scriptures. Experience alone is not a sound guide. You must be cautious about isolating a single experience from the context of Scripture. You will never go wrong if, under the Holy Spirit's instruction, you let the Bible be your guide.

The Bible Is Your Guide

The Bible is the Christian's guide. How do we let the Word of God be our guide? When I seek God's direction, I insist on following the guidelines that I see in the Word of God. Yesterday's lesson is an example. Does God call people to follow Him without giving them all the details up front? We know that He called Abram to follow that way. Is that pattern consistent in the Scriptures?

Read the following Scriptures about God's (Jesus') call for people to follow Him. Write the names of those who were called to follow without being given much detail about what the future would hold for them.

1. Matthew 4:18-20 _____
2. Matthew 4:21-22 _____
3. Matthew 9:9 _____
4. Acts 9:1-20 _____

In some cases God gave more details than in others. For Moses and the children of Israel, God provided daily guidance through the cloud by day and the fire by night. For Peter, Andrew, James, John, Matthew, and Paul (answers to the above activity), God gave very little details about their assignment. He basically said, "Just follow Me, and I will show you." In every case, however, the individuals had to stay close to God for daily guidance.

What Is God's Will for My Life?

When people seek to know and do the will of God, many ask the question, What is God's will for my life? A seminary professor of mine, Dr. Gaines S. Dobbins, used to say, "If you ask the wrong question, you are going to get the wrong answer." Always check to see if you have asked the right question.

The right question is: What is God's will?

What is God's will for my life? is *not* the right question. I think the right question is, What is God's will? In other words, what is it that God is purposing where I am. Once I know what God is doing, then I know what I need to do. The focus needs to be on *God,* not *my life!*

Jesus' Example

When I want to learn how to know and do the will of God, I can find no better model than Jesus. He perfectly completed every assignment that God gave Him to do. He never failed to do the will of the Father. He never sinned. Would you like to understand how Jesus came to know and do the will of God?

"My Father is always at his work to this very day, and I, too, am working.

"I tell you the truth, the Son can do nothing by himself; he can do only what he sees his Father doing, because whatever the Father does the Son also does. For the Father loves the Son and shows him all he does. Yes, to your amazement he will show him even greater things than these."

—John 5:17, 19-20

 Read John 5:17, 19-20 (left) and answer the following questions.

1. Who is always at work? _____
2. How much can the Son do by Himself? _____
3. What does the Son do? _____
4. Why does the Father show the Son what He is doing? _____

_____

The verses you just read contain the clearest statements of how Jesus knew what to do. I would outline Jesus' approach to knowing and doing God's will like this:

Jesus' Example

- The Father has been working right up until now.
- Now God has Me working.
- I do nothing on My own initiative.
- I watch to see what the Father is doing.
- I do what I see the Father already is doing.
- You see, the Father loves Me.
- He shows Me everything that He, Himself, is doing.

This model is for your life personally and for your church. It is not just a step-by-step approach for knowing and doing the will of God. It describes a love relationship through which God accomplishes His purposes. I would sum it up this way: Watch to see where God is working and join Him!

God Is Always at Work Around You

Right now God is working all around you and in your life. One of the greatest tragedies among God's people is that, while they have a deep longing to experience God, they are experiencing God day after day but do not know how to recognize Him. By the end of this course, you will have learned many ways to recognize clearly the activity of God in and around your life. The Holy Spirit and the Word of God will instruct you and help you know when and where God is working. Once you know where He is working, you will adjust your life to join Him where He is working.

When you enter this kind of intimate love relationship with God, you will know and do the will of God and experience Him in ways you have never known Him before. You will experience His accomplishing His activity through your life. I cannot accomplish that goal in your life. Only God can bring you into that kind of relationship.

 Turn to the diagram inside the back cover of this book. Read all seven of the realities of experiencing God. Make the first statement personal by writing it below, using *me* instead of *you*.

_____

Later this week, we will take a closer look at these seven truths.

 Review today's lesson. Pray and ask God to identify one or more statements or Scriptures that He wants you to understand, learn, or practice. Then respond to the following:

What was the most meaningful statement or Scripture you read today?

_____

Reword the statement or Scripture into a prayer of response to God.

_____

_____

What does God want you to do in response to today's study?

_____

SUMMARY STATEMENTS

- I will look to see what God says and how He works in the Scriptures.
  I will make my decisions and evaluate my experiences based on biblical principles.
- The Bible is my guide for faith and practice.
- The right question is, What is God's will?
- I will watch to see where God is working and join Him.
- God is always at work around me.

Watch to see where God is working and join Him!

LEARNING TO BE A SERVANT OF GOD

To be a servant of God you must be moldable and remain in the hand of the Master.

What Is a Servant?

Many Scripture passages describe Jesus as God's Servant. Here is what Paul said about Him:

> Your attitude should be the same as that of Christ Jesus: Who, being in very nature God, did not consider equality with God something to be grasped, but made himself nothing, taking the very nature of a servant (Phil. 2:5-7).

In His instructions to His disciples about servanthood, Jesus (the Son of man) described His own role of service:

> "Whoever wants to become great among you must be your servant, and whoever wants to be first must be your slave—just as the Son of Man did not come to be served, but to serve" (Matt. 20:26-28).

Jesus also told us about our relationship to Him: "As the Father has sent me, I am sending you" (John 20:21).

 What is a servant? In your own words write a definition of a servant.

_____

Did your definition of _servant_ sound something like this: "A servant is one who finds out what his master wants him to do and then does it"? The world's concept of a servant is that a servant goes to the master and says, "Master, what do you want me to do?" The master tells him, and the servant goes off by himself and does it. That is not a biblical concept of a servant.

Like the potter and the clay

My understanding of a servant is more like the potter and the clay. (See Jer. 18:1-6.) The clay has to do two things. First of all, the clay has to be molded. It has to be responsive to the potter, so the potter can make any instrument of his choosing. Then the clay has to do a second thing–remain in the potter's hand.

Suppose the potter molds the clay into a cup. The cup has to remain in the potter's hands, so the potter can use that cup in any way he chooses. When you come to God as His servant, He first wants you to allow Him to mold and shape you into the instrument of His choosing. Then He can take your life and put it where He wills and work through it to accomplish His purposes.

 Answer the following questions about being a servant.

1. How much can a servant do by himself or herself?_____

2. When God works through a servant, how much can that servant do?

_____

3. What are two things a servant must do to be used by God?

_____

_____

"This is the word that came to Jeremiah from the Lord: 'Go down to the potter's house, and there I will give you my message.' So I went down to the potter's house, and I saw him working at the wheel. But the pot he was shaping from the clay was marred in his hands; so the potter formed it into another pot, shaping it as seemed best to him.

"Then the word of the Lord came to me: 'O house of Israel, can I not do with you as this potter does?' declares the LORD. 'Like clay in the hand of the potter, so are you in my hand, O house of Israel.'"

—Jeremiah 18:1-6

A servant has to: (1) be moldable and (2) remain in the Master's (potter's) hands. The servant can do nothing of Kingdom value by himself or herself.

If you have been working by the world's definition of servant, this concept should change your approach to serving God. You do not get orders and then go out and do them. You relate to God, respond to Him, and adjust your life to Him so that He can do whatever He wants to do through you.

Elijah Was God's Servant

When Elijah challenged the prophets of Baal (a Canaanite fertility god) to prove whose God was the true God, he took a big risk in being a servant of God.

 Read 1 Kings 18:16-39 and answer the following questions.

1. How many prophets of other gods did Elijah face at Mount Carmel?_____

2. What was the test Elijah proposed to prove who was the One True God?

_____

3. What did Elijah do to the altar of the Lord?

_____

4. At whose initiative did Elijah offer this challenge? His own or God's?

_____

5. What did he plan to prove through this experience?

_____

6. How did all the people respond? _____

7. What was God's work in this event? _____

_____

8. What was Elijah's work in this event?_____

Elijah was outnumbered 850 to 1. If God had not displayed His own work by consuming the sacrifice (and altar) as Elijah had proposed, Elijah would have utterly failed. That would probably have cost him his life. Elijah went where God told him, when God told him, and did what God told him. Then God accomplished His own purposes through him. Elijah wanted the people to identify the Lord as the True God. That is exactly how the people responded.

Outnumbered

Did Elijah or God bring down the fire from Heaven? God did. What was Elijah doing? Being obedient. Elijah had no ability to do what God was about to do. When God did something only He could do, all the people knew that He was the True God. And God did it through His obedient servant.

Reflection Time

 As your study time permits, read the following thought-provoking questions. Try to mentally answer each one before moving to the next one. You may want to jot a note to yourself on the response lines.

1. What differences will there be between the quality of service and the quantity of lasting results when God is working and when you are working?

_____

2. What are you doing in your life personally and in your church that you know cannot be accomplished unless God intervenes?

_____

3. When we finish a task and feel frustrated that lasting spiritual fruit is not visible, could the reason be we are attempting very little only God can do?

_____

"Don't Just Do Something"

We are a "doing" people. We always want to be doing something. Once in a while someone will say, "Don't just stand there, do something."

I think God is crying out and shouting to us, "Don't just do something. Stand there! Enter into a love relationship with Me. Get to know Me. Adjust your life to Me. Let Me love you and reveal Myself to you as I work through you." A time will come when the doing will be called for, but we cannot skip the relationship. The relationship with God must come first.

Jesus said, "I am the vine; you are the branches. If a man remains in me and I in him, he will bear much fruit; apart from me you can do nothing" (John 15:5). Do you believe Him? Without Him you can do nothing. He means that.

 Turn to the diagram inside the back cover of this book. Read again all seven of the realities listed there. Personalize the last (seventh) reality and write it below using _I_ and _me_ instead of _you_.

_____

Find out where the Master is, then that is where you need to be.

Do you want to be a servant of God? Find out where the Master is. That is where you need to be. Find out what the Master is doing. That is what you need to be doing. Jesus said: "Whoever serves me must follow me; and where I am, my servant also will be. My Father will honor the one who serves me" (John 12:26).

 Review today's lesson. Pray and ask God to identify one or more statements or Scriptures that He wants you to understand, learn, or practice. Then respond to the following:

What was the most meaningful statement or Scripture you read today?

_____

Reword the statement or Scripture into a prayer of response to God.

_____

What does God want you to do in response to today's study?

_____

Practice quoting your Scripture memory verse aloud and/or writing it.

SUMMARY STATEMENTS

- To be a servant of God I must be moldable and I must remain in the Master's hand.
- Apart from God, I can do nothing.
- With God working through me, I can do anything God can do.
- When I find out where the Master is, then I know that is where I need to be.
- I come to know God by experience as I obey Him and He accomplishes His work through me.

GOD WORKS THROUGH HIS SERVANTS, PART 1

You cannot stay the way you are and go with God.

We often act as though God tells us what He wants us to do and then sends us off all by ourselves to try to do it. Then, anytime we need Him, we can call on Him; and He will help us. That is never the biblical picture. When God is about to do something, He reveals to His people what He is about to do. He wants to do His work through His people, or through His servant.

When God is about to do something through you, He has to get you from where you are to where He is. So He comes and tells you what He is doing. (Later, I will try to help you understand how you can clearly know when God is speaking to you.) When you know what God is doing, then you know what you need to do—you need to join Him. The moment you know that God is doing something where you are, your life will be thrown in contrast to God. You cannot stay the way you are and go with God.

Seven Realities of Experiencing God

The seven realities illustration inside the back cover of your book will help you summarize the way you can respond to God's leadership in your life. Study that illustration right now.

Here are the seven realities in statement form:
1. God is always at work around you.
2. God pursues a continuing love relationship with you that is real and personal.
3. God invites you to become involved with Him in His work.
4. God speaks by the Holy Spirit through the Bible, prayer, circumstances, and the church to reveal Himself, His purposes, and His ways.
5. God's invitation for you to work with Him always leads you to a crisis of belief that requires faith and action.
6. You must make major adjustments in your life to join God in what He is doing.
7. You come to know God by experience as you obey Him, and He accomplishes His work through you.

A. Circle key words or phrases that help you recall the seven realities.

B. Write the key words or phrases on the following lines:

_____

_____

_____

_____

C. Read each reality slowly. Write below any questions you have about any of the realities you do not quite understand.

_____

_____

_____

D. Using only the words or phrases you wrote in item B, see if you can mentally summarize all seven of the realities. Check yourself before moving on to the next activity in this exercise.

E. Now, on a separate sheet of paper, try writing each of the realities from memory. They do not have to be word-for-word, but they should cover the important information of the realities.

Most of this course will focus on one or more of these realities to help you understand them more completely. You will probably notice that I frequently repeat different aspects of this cycle. I use the repetition in different situations to help you learn how you can respond to God's activity in your life.

In the assignment above you could have selected many different words or phrases. Yours may be different, but I chose *God/work; love relationship; involved with Him; God speaks; crisis of belief; adjustments; obey*. You may have asked questions like:
• What is involved in a love relationship with God?
• How can I know when God is speaking?
• How do I know where God is at work?
• What kinds of adjustments does God require me to make?
• What is the difference between adjustment and obedience?

As I have worked with groups and individuals in many settings, I have been asked questions like these. I will try to answer as many questions during the remaining units of this course as I possibly can. I will answer many other questions in the optional videotaped messages that go along with this course.

Three similarities in the lives of Bible characters through whom God worked are:
• When God spoke, they knew it was God.
• They knew what God was saying.
• They knew what they were to do in response to what God said.

Wouldn't you like for God to work through you that way? He wants to move you into that kind of relationship. I trust that this course will help you.

Moses' Example

Moses' call and ministry are good examples of how God worked with persons in the Bible. His early life and call to ministry are described in chapters 2, 3, and 4 of Exodus. Other passages of Scripture also help us see how Moses came to know and follow God's will. Using the seven points in the sequence of realities related to experiencing God, let's look at Moses' call and response. (You may want to read Ex. 2—4 as a background passage.)

Reality 1: God already was at work around Moses.

> The Israelites groaned in their slavery and cried out, and their cry for help because of their slavery went up to God. God heard their groaning and he remembered his covenant with Abraham, with Isaac and with Jacob. So God looked on the Israelites and was concerned about them (Ex. 2:23-25).

Reality 2: God pursued a continuing love relationship with Moses that was real and personal.

God took the initiative or "first step" to come to Moses and establish a love relationship with him at the burning bush. God told Moses that He would go with him into Egypt. Many passages throughout Exodus, Leviticus, Numbers, and Deuteronomy illustrate how God pursued a continuing love relationship with Moses. Here are two examples:

Reality 3: God invited Moses to become involved with Him in His work.

> I have come down to rescue them [the Israelites] from the hand of the Egyptians and to bring them up out of that land into a good and spacious land. . . . So now, go. I am sending you to Pharaoh to bring my people the Israelites out of Egypt (Ex. 3:8, 10).

The Lord said to Moses, "Come up to me on the mountain and stay here, and I will give you the tablets of stone, with the law and commands I have written for their [the Israelites] instruction". . . .

When Moses went up on the mountain, the cloud covered it, and the glory of the Lord settled on Mount Sinai. . . . Moses entered the cloud as he went on up the mountain. And he stayed on the mountain forty days and forty nights (Ex. 24:12, 15-16, 18).

 Answer the following questions about the first three realities.

1. Related to Israel, what was God already doing?

_____

2. How did God want to involve Moses in the work He was already doing?

_____

3. What evidence do you see that proves God wanted a personal and real relationship with Moses?

_____

(1) God had a purpose that He was working out in Moses' world. Even though Moses was an exile in the desert, he was right on God's schedule, right in the fullness of God's timing, right in the middle of God's will. At the time God was about to deliver the children of Israel from slavery in Egypt. The important factor was not what the will of God was for Moses. The important factor was what the will of God was for Israel. (2) God's purpose was to deliver the children of Israel. Moses was the one through whom God wanted to work to accomplish that. (3) Time and time again God invited Moses to talk with Him and to be with Him. God established and maintained a continuing relationship with Moses. This relationship was based on love. Daily God fulfilled His purposes through His "friend" Moses. (For other examples of the love relationship, you may want to read Ex. 33:7–34:10 or Num. 12:6-8.)

Whenever God gets ready to do something, He always reveals to a person or His people what He is going to do. (See Amos 3:7.) God accomplishes His work through His people. This is the way God works with you. The Bible is designed to help you understand the ways of God. Then, when God starts to act in your life, you will recognize that it is God.

"Surely the Sovereign Lord does nothing without revealing his plan to his servants the prophets."

—Amos 3:7

 Review today's lesson. Pray and ask God to identify one or more statements or Scriptures that He wants you to understand, learn, or practice. Then respond to the following:

What was the most meaningful statement or Scripture you read today?

_____

Reword the statement or Scripture into a prayer of response to God.

_____

_____

What does God want you to do in response to today's study?

_____

Since this is a two-part lesson, we will begin with statement 4 tomorrow. This two-part lesson will be summarized at the end of Day 5.

GOD WORKS THROUGH HIS SERVANTS, PART 2

God reveals what He is about to do. That revelation becomes an invitation to join Him.

God's Invitation

Yesterday, you studied the first three realities of God's working with Moses. Now we'll look at the last four. Reality 4 emphasizes that God spoke to reveal Himself, His purposes, and His ways to Moses:

Reality 4: God spoke to reveal Himself, His purposes, and His ways.

> There the angel of the Lord appeared to him in flames of fire from within a bush. . . . God called to him from within the bush, "Moses! Moses!". . . . And Moses said, "Here I am."
> "Do not come any closer," God said. "Take off your sandals, for the place where you are standing is holy ground." Then he said, "I am the God of your father, the God of Abraham, the God of Isaac and the God of Jacob."
> The Lord said, "I have indeed seen the misery of my people in Egypt. I have heard them crying out because of their slave drivers, and I am concerned about their suffering. So I have come down to rescue them from the hand of the Egyptians and to bring them up out of that land into a good and spacious land" (Ex. 3:2-8).

Moses revealed his crisis of belief when he responded to God's invitation:

Reality 5: God's invitation for Moses to work with Him led to a crisis of belief that required faith and action.

> "Who am I, that I should go to Pharaoh and bring the Israelites out of Egypt? . . . Suppose I go to the Israelites and say to them, 'The God of your fathers has sent me to you,' and they ask me, 'What is his name?' Then what shall I tell them?" (Ex. 3:11, 13)
> "What if they do not believe me or listen to me and say, 'The Lord did not appear to you'? . . . O Lord, I have never been eloquent, neither in the past nor since you have spoken to your servant. I am slow of speech and tongue (Ex. 4:1, 10).
> "O Lord, please send someone else to do it" (Ex. 4:13).

Moses' crisis called for faith and action:

Reality 6: Moses had to make major adjustments in his life to join God in what He was doing.

> By faith Moses, when he had grown up, refused to be known as the son of Pharaoh's daughter. He chose to be mistreated along with the people of God rather than to enjoy the pleasures of sin for a short time. . . . By faith he left Egypt, not fearing the king's anger; he persevered because he saw him who is invisible. By faith he kept the Passover and the sprinkling of blood, so that the destroyer of the firstborn would not touch the firstborn of Israel. By faith the people passed through the Red Sea as on dry land; but when the Egyptians tried to do so, they were drowned (Heb. 11:24-29).

Reality 7: Moses came to know God by experience as he obeyed God and God accomplished His work through Moses.

As Moses obeyed God, God accomplished through Moses what Moses could not do. Here is one example when Moses and the people came to know God as their Deliverer:

> Then the Lord said to Moses, "Why are you crying out to me? Tell the Israelites to move on. Raise your staff and stretch out your hand over the sea to divide the water so that the Israelites can go through the sea on dry ground. . . . Then Moses stretched out his hand over the sea, and all that night the Lord drove the sea back with a strong east

wind and turned it into dry land. The waters were divided, and the Israelites went through the sea on dry ground, with a wall of water on their right and on their left. . . . And when the Israelites saw the great power the Lord displayed against the Egyptians, the people feared the Lord and put their trust in him and in Moses his servant (Ex. 14:15-16, 21-22, 31).

 Answer the following questions about realities four through seven.

1. What did God reveal about Himself, His purposes, and His ways?

_____

2. What did Moses have trouble believing about God?

_____

3. How would you summarize Moses' faith as described in Hebrews 11?

_____

4. What adjustment(s) did Moses have to make?

_____

5. How do you think Moses must have felt when God delivered the Israelites through him?

_____

(1) God revealed to Moses His holiness, His mercy, His power, His name, His purpose to keep His promise to Abraham and give Israel the promised land, and many other things not described in the Scriptures you just read. (2) Moses questioned whether God could do the task through him (Ex. 3:11), whether the Israelites would believe God had appeared to him (Ex. 4:1); and whether he was capable of speaking eloquently enough to get the job done (Ex. 4:10). In each case Moses was really doubting God more than himself. He faced the crisis of belief—Is God really able to do what He says? (3) Moses' faith is described in Hebrews 11:24-29 as a model of self-sacrifice and trust in an Almighty God. (4) Moses had to come to the place where he believed God could do everything He said He would do. Then he had to move to Egypt. After making these adjustments, he was in a position where he could obey God. (5) Moses must have felt humility and unworthiness to be used in such a significant way. Every step of obedience brought Moses (and Israel) to a greater knowledge of God (Ex. 6:1-8).

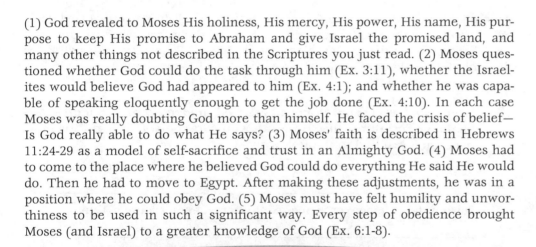

God reveals what He is about to do. That revelation becomes an invitation to join Him.

What Can One "Ordinary" Person Do?

When God healed the crippled beggar through Peter, he and John were called before the Sanhedrin, the Jewish ruling body, to give an account of their actions. Filled with the Holy Spirit, Peter spoke boldly to the religious leaders. Notice their response: "When they saw the courage of Peter and John and realized that they were unschooled, *ordinary men*, they were astonished and they took note that these men had been with Jesus" (Acts 4:13).

Peter and John

Uneducated but Mighty

All of the persons that you see in the Scriptures were ordinary people. Their relationship with God and the activity of God is what made them extraordinary. Anyone who will take the time to enter into an intimate relationship with God can see God do extraordinary things through his or her life.

From shoe salesman to flaming evangelist

Dwight L. Moody was a poorly educated shoe salesman who felt the call of God to preach the gospel. He was an ordinary man who sought to be fully and wholly consecrated to Christ. Through this one ordinary life, God began to do the extraordinary. Moody became one of the greatest evangelists of modern times.

 Could God work in extraordinary ways through your life to accomplish significant things for His kingdom? Yes ❑ No ❑

When you believe that nothing significant can happen through you, you have said more about your belief in God than you have said about yourself.

You might say, "Well, I am not a D. L. Moody." You don't have to be a D. L. Moody. God doesn't want you to be a D. L. Moody. God wants you to be you and let Him do through you whatever He chooses. When you believe that nothing significant can happen through you, you have said that God is not capable of doing anything significant through you. The truth is He is able to do anything He pleases with one ordinary person fully dedicated to Him.

God's Standards Are Different

Don't be surprised that God's standards of excellence are different from those of the world. How long was the public ministry of John the Baptist? Perhaps six months. What was Jesus' estimate of John's life? He said, "I tell you, among those born of women there is no one greater than John" (Luke 7:28). None greater! John had six months wholly yielded to God, and the Son of God put that stamp of approval on his life.

John the Baptist

"None Greater"

If you feel weak, limited, ordinary, you are the best material through which God can work.

An ordinary person is the one God most likes to use. Paul noted that God deliberately seeks out the weak things and the despised things because it is from them that He can receive the greatest glory (1 Cor. 1:26-31). Then everyone will know that only God could have done the work. If you feel weak, limited, ordinary, you are the best material through which God can work.

 Review today's lesson. Pray and ask God to identify one or more statements or Scriptures that He wants you to understand, learn, or practice. Then respond to the following:

What was the most meaningful statement or Scripture you read today?

_____

Reword the statement or Scripture into a prayer of response to God.

_____

What does God want you to do in response to today's study?

_____

Review your Scripture memory verse and be prepared to recite it to a partner in your small-group session this week.

SUMMARY STATEMENTS

- God reveals what He is about to do.
- The revelation becomes an invitation to join Him.
- I can't stay the way I am and go with God.
- God is able to do anything He pleases with one ordinary person fully dedicated to Him.
- God's standards of excellence are different from the world's.

LOOKING TO GOD

SUMMER YOUTH CAMP

As they made plans to attend summer youth camp, Jeremy and Tim prayed that the Lord would work through them to help others. So, when they arrived at camp, they began to watch and see what persons God brought into their path.

While checking in they met Brad, whose aunt was one of the program personalities for the week. At the last minute she had asked him to come along and watch her children during her performances. The moment they met Brad, Tim and Jeremy had a feeling that God wanted to involve them in doing a work in his life. They made every effort to "bump" into Brad.

At first, Brad seemed cold when Tim or Jeremy tried to strike up a conversation with him. That was discouraging. Then somebody told Tim that Brad played a guitar. He and Jeremy decided to ask Brad to join them in playing their guitars each night. Through their conversations during these "jam sessions," Brad discovered that his present life-style of drinking, drugs, and partying was similar to Jeremy's past. Because of these similar experiences, Brad felt that he could talk to Jeremy and Tim about his problems. That opened the door for several conversations, including a lunch that, unfortunately, turned into a "tag-team" witnessing match, ending in a draw.

When Jeremy and Tim left camp, Brad had not accepted Christ, as far as they knew. And they really did not expect to hear from him again. But, at Christmas, Jeremy got a card from Brad. The note inside went like this:

> Merry Christmas! This is a special Christmas for me, because it will be the first Christmas with Jesus in my heart. I only had Him in my head until that day I had lunch with you and Tim. I thank God for you two—sometimes in tears—because of how He used you to explain salvation and grace to me in a way I had never known before....
>
> You're the first real friends I've ever had. When you looked me in the eye and told me exactly what I was feeling, what kind of person I was, how to deal with my fears and my problems, it was all too much. I knew God had sent you, and I could deny Him no longer. He saved me! Happy New Year!

Jeremy and Tim looked to see where God was working and joined Him. What a difference that made!

Some trust in chariots and some in horses, but we trust in the name of the Lord our God.

—PSALM 20:7

GOD-CENTERED LIVING

To know and do the will of God, you must deny self and return to a God-centered life.

Self-centered Versus God-Centered

Part of the Book of Genesis is the record of God accomplishing His purposes through Abraham. It is not the record of Abraham's walk with God. Can you see the difference in focus? The focus of the Bible is God. The essence of sin is a shift from a God-centeredness to a self-centeredness. The essence of salvation is a denial of self, not an affirming of self. We must come to a denial of self and a return to a God-centeredness with our lives. Then God can accomplish through us purposes He had before He created the world. Though more could be said, here are some descriptions of the life orientations available to you:

Self-centered:
- Life focused on self
- Overly proud of self and self's accomplishments
- Depending on self and one's own abilities
- Seeking to be acceptable to the world and its ways
- Looking at circumstances from a human perspective

God-centered:
- Confidence in God
- Dependence on God and His ability and provision
- Life focused on God and His activity
- Humble before God
- Denying self
- Seeking first the kingdom of God and His righteousness
- Seeking God's viewpoint in every circumstance
- Holy and godly living

 In your own words write a definition of the following:

Self-centered _____

God-centered _____

In each of the following pairs of biblical examples, write a *G* before the one that illustrates God-centeredness. Write an *S* before the one that illustrates self-centeredness.

___ 1a. God placed Adam and Eve in a beautiful and fertile garden. He told them not to eat from the tree of the knowledge of good and evil. Eve saw that the fruit of the tree was pleasing to the eye and desirable for gaining wisdom, so she ate it (Gen. 2:16-17; 3:1-7).

___ 1b. Potiphar's wife daily begged Joseph to come to bed with her. He told her he could not do such a wicked thing and sin against God. When she tried to force him, he ran from the room. He went to prison rather than yield to temptation (Gen. 39).

God had promised to give the land of Canaan to Israel. Moses sent 12 men into the Promised Land to explore it and bring back a report. The land was fertile, but the people living there were seen as giants (Num. 13—14).

___ 2a. Ten of the spies said, "We can't attack those people; they are stronger than we are" (13:31).

___ 2b. Joshua and Caleb said, "If the Lord is pleased with us, he will lead us into that land, a land flowing with milk and honey, and will give it to us. Only do not rebel against the lord. And do not be afraid of the people of the land" (14:8, 9).

___ 3a. King Asa was facing the army of Zerah the Cushite. He said, "Lord, there is no one like you to help the powerless against the mighty. Help us, O Lord our God, for we rely on you, and in your name we have come against this vast army. O Lord, you are our God; do not let man prevail against you" (2 Chron. 14:9-11).

___ 3b. King Asa and Judah were being threatened by Baasha, king of Israel. Asa sent gold and silver from the temple and his own palace to Ben-Hadad king of Aram asking for his help in this conflict (2 Chron. 16:1-3).

Self-centeredness is a subtle trap. It makes so much sense (humanly speaking). Like King Asa you can avoid it at one time and fall right into the trap at another time. God-centeredness requires a daily denial of self and submission to God (John 12:23-25). Illustrations of God-centeredness are 1-b, 2-b, 3-a. The others illustrate self-centeredness.

God's Purposes Not Our Plans

To live a God-centered life, you must focus your life on God's purposes not your own plans. You must seek to see from God's viewpoint rather than from your own distorted human viewpoint. When God starts to do something in the world, He takes the initiative to come and talk to somebody. For some divine reason, He has chosen to involve His people in accomplishing His purposes.

 Answer the following questions. Read the Scriptures listed if you do not already know the answer.

1. What was GOD about to do when He came to Noah and asked him to build an ark? (Gen. 6:5-14)

_____

2. What was GOD about to do to Sodom and Gomorrah when He came to Abraham? (Gen. 18:16-21; 19:13)

_____

3. What was GOD about to do when He came to Gideon? (Judg. 6:11-16)

_____

4. What was GOD about to do when He came to Saul (later called Paul) on the road to Damascus? (Acts 9:1-16)

_____

5. At each of these moments, what was the most important factor? **Check one.**

❏ What the individual wanted to do for God

❏ What GOD was about to do

God was about to destroy the world with a flood when He came to Noah. When God prepared to destroy Sodom and Gomorrah, He came to tell Abraham about it. God came to Gideon when He was about to deliver the Israelites from the oppression of Midian. God came to Saul (Paul) when He was ready to take the gospel message to the Gentiles around the known world. Without a doubt, the most important factor in each situation was what God was about to do.

Let's use Noah for an example. What about all the plans he had to serve God? They would not make much sense in light of the coming destruction, would they? Noah was not calling God in to help him accomplish what he was

"Unless a kernel of wheat falls to the ground and dies, it remains only a single seed. But if it dies, it produces many seeds. The man who loves his life will lose it, while the man who hates his life in this world will keep it for eternal life."
—John 12:23-25

You never find God asking persons to dream up what they want to do for Him.

dreaming he was going to do for God. You never find God asking persons to dream up what they want to do for Him.

Submit
Wait
Watch
Join

We do not sit down and dream what we want to do for God and then call God in to help us accomplish it. The pattern in the Scripture is that we submit ourselves to God and:
• We wait until God shows us what He is about to do, or
• we watch to see what God is doing around us and join Him.

 Review today's lesson. Pray and ask God to identify one or more statements or Scriptures that He wants you to understand, learn, or practice. Underline them. Then respond to the following:

What was the most meaningful statement or Scripture you read today?

_____

_____

Reword the statement or Scripture into a prayer of response to God.

_____

_____

What does God want you to do in response to today's study?

_____

_____

Write your Scripture memory verse for this week on the following lines. Remember, you may select a different verse.

_____

_____

Review your memory verse from last week.

SUMMARY STATEMENTS
• To know and do the will of God, I must deny self and return to a God-centered life.
• I must reorient my life to God.
• I must focus my life on God's purposes, not my own plans.
• I must seek to see from God's perspective rather than from my own distorted human perspective.
• I must wait until God shows me what He is about to do through me.
• I will watch to see what God is doing around me and join Him.

GOD'S PLANS VERSUS OUR PLANS

Who delivered the children of Israel from Egypt? Moses or God? God did. God chose to bring Moses into a relationship with Himself so that He—God—could deliver Israel. Did Moses ever try to take matters into his own hands? Yes.

In Exodus 2:11-15 (right margin) Moses began to assert himself in behalf of his own people. But Moses tried to take Israelite matters into his own hands. That cost him 40 years of exile in Midian working as a shepherd (and reorienting his life to God-centered living).

What might have happened if Moses had tried to deliver the children of Israel through a human approach? Thousands would have been slain. When God delivered the Israelites, how many were lost? None. In the process God even led the Egyptians to give the Israelites their gold, silver, and clothes. Egypt was plundered, the Egyptian army was destroyed, and the Israelites did not lose a single person (see Ex. 14:15-31).

Why don't we realize that it is always best to do things God's way? We cause some of the wreck and ruin in our churches because we have a plan. We carry out the plan and get out of it only what we can do. God (Jesus) is the head over the body—the church. Oh, that we would discover the difference when we let God be the Head of that body. He will accomplish more in six months through a people yielded to Him than we could do in 60 years without Him.

God's Ways

 Read the following Scripture and look for God's response to those who will not follow His ways. Then answer the questions that follow.

> "I am the Lord your God, who brought you up out of Egypt. Open wide your mouth and I will fill it. But my people would not listen to me; Israel would not submit to me. So I gave them over to their stubborn hearts to follow their own devices" (Ps. 81:10-12).

1. What had God already done for Israel? _____

2. What did God promise to His people? _____

3. How did the people respond? _____

4. What did God do? _____

Now read the next two verses to see what could have been true for Israel. Then answer the question that follows.

> "'If my people would but listen to me, if Israel would follow my ways, how quickly would I subdue their enemies and turn my hand against their foes!'" (Ps. 81:13-14).

5. What could have been true if Israel had listened to and followed God?

_____

Read Hebrews 3:7-19. Then answer one more question.

6. Why were many of the Israelites denied entrance to the promised land?

_____

"One day, after Moses had grown up, he went out to where his own people were and watched them at their hard labor. He saw an Egyptian beating a Hebrew, one of his own people. Glancing this way and that and seeing no one, he killed the Egyptian and hid him in the sand. The next day he went out and saw two Hebrews fighting. He asked the one in the wrong, 'Why are you hitting your fellow Hebrew?'

"The man said, 'Who made you ruler and judge over us? Are you thinking of killing me as you killed the Egyptian?' Then Moses was afraid and thought, 'What I did must have become known.'

"When Pharaoh heard of this, he tried to kill Moses, but Moses fled from Pharaoh and went to live in Midian."
—Exodus 2:11-15

God brought Israel out of Egypt with many miraculous signs and wonders. So, wouldn't you think they could trust God to do just about anything? That's not what happened, though. When the Israelites got to the promised land, they did not trust Him to deliver the promised land to them. For that reason, they spent the next 40 years wandering in the wilderness. In Psalm 81, God reminded Israel that He would have conquered their enemies *quickly* if they had only followed His plans rather than their own devices.

 Think about and answer the following questions:

1. Has God changed in the way He works with people to carry out His plans and purposes?

   _____

2. Would you rather follow your own plans and wander around in a spiritual wilderness or follow God's ways and quickly enter a spiritual promised land? Give a reason for your answer.

   _____

   _____

We are His servants, and we adjust our lives to what He is about to do.

We adjust our lives to God so He can do through us what He wants to do. God is not our servant to make adjustment to our plans. We are His servants, and we adjust our lives to what He is about to do. If we will not submit, God will let us follow our own devices. In following them, however, we will never experience what God is waiting and wanting to do in our behalf or through us for others.

You Need to Know What God Is About to Do

When God called the prophets, He often had a two-fold message. The first desire of God was: "Call the people to return to Me." If the people failed to respond, they needed to hear the second message: "Let them know that they are closer to the moment of judgment than they have ever been." God's word to the prophet was, "Tell the people: This is what I have been doing. This is what I am doing right now. This is what I am about to do. Then call them to respond."

> Understanding what God is about to do where you are is more important than telling God what you want to do for Him.

You need to know what God has on His agenda for your church, community, and nation at this time in history. Then you and your church can adjust your lives to God, so that He can move you into the mainstream of His activity. Though God likely will not give you a detailed schedule, He will let you know one step at a time how you and your church need to respond to what He is doing.

 Pray right now and ask for God's guidance on how you should respond to Him . . .

- in your personal life
- in your family
- in your church
- in your school or work
- in your community
- in our nation

You may want to jot some notes in the margin or on a separate piece of paper.

What was God about to do when He started to tell Martin Luther that "the just shall live by faith"? He was going to bring people all over Europe to an understanding that salvation was a free gift and that each person had direct access to Him. He was bringing about a great Reformation. As you study great movements of God in church history, you will notice in every case that God came to someone and the person released his life to God. Then God began to accomplish His purposes through that individual.

When God began to speak to John and Charles Wesley, He was preparing for a sweeping revival in England that saved England from a bloody revolution like France had experienced. There stood a couple of men, along with George Whitfield and some others, through whom God was able to do a mighty work and turn England completely around.

In your community some things are about to happen in the lives of others. God wants to intercept those lives. Suppose He wants to do it through you. He comes to you and talks to you. But you are so self-centered, you respond, "I don't think I am trained. I don't think I am able to do it. And I . . ."

Do you see what happens? The focus is on self. The moment you sense that God is moving in your life, you give Him a list of reasons why He has selected the wrong person or why the time is not right (Ex. 3:11; 4:1). I wish you would seek God's viewpoint. God knows you can't do it! But He wants to do it Himself *through* you.

Review today's lesson. Pray and ask God to identify one or more statements or Scriptures that He wants you to understand, learn, or practice. Underline them. Then respond to the following:

What was the most meaningful statement or Scripture you read today?

_____

Reword the statement or Scripture into a prayer of response to God.

_____

_____

What does God want you to do in response to today's study?

_____

SUMMARY STATEMENTS

- Do things God's way.
- God will accomplish more in six months through a people yielded to Him than we could do in 60 years without Him.
- I am God's servant. I adjust my life to what He is about to do.
- Understanding what God is about to do where I am is more important than telling God what I want to do for Him.

Martin Luther

John and Charles Wesley

George Whitfield

GOD TAKES THE FIRST STEP

God's revelation of His activity is an invitation for you to join Him.

God's Initiative Not Yours

All the way through the Scripture, God takes the initiative. When He comes to a person, He always reveals Himself and His activity. That revelation is an invitation for the individual to adjust his life to God. None of the people God ever encountered could remain the same after the encounter. They had to make major adjustments in their lives in order to walk obediently with God.

"It is God who works in you to will and to act according to his good purpose."
—*Philippians 2:13*

God is the Sovereign Lord. I try to keep my life God-centered because He is the One who is the Pace Setter. He is always the One to take the initiative to accomplish what He wants to do. When you are God-centered, even the desires to do the things that please God come from God's initiative in your life (Phil. 2:13).

What often happens when we see God at work? We immediately get self-centered rather than God-centered. Somehow we must reorient our lives to God. We must learn to see things from His viewpoint. We must allow Him to develop His character in us. We must let Him reveal His thoughts to us. Only then can we get a proper perspective on life.

If you keep your life God-centered, you will put your life alongside His activity. When you see God at work around you, your heart will leap within you and say, "Thank You, Father, thank You for letting me be involved where You are." When I am in the middle of the activity of God and God opens my eyes to let me see where He is working, I always assume that God wants me to join Him.

Answer the following questions by checking your responses.

1. Who takes the initiative in your knowing and doing the will of God?

   ❏ a. I do. God waits on me until I decide what I want to do for Him.

   ❏ b. God does. He invites me to join Him in what He is about to do.

2. Which of the following are ways God may reveal His plan or purpose to you? **Check all that apply.**

   ❏ a. He lets me see where He is already working around me.

   ❏ b. He speaks to me through Scripture and impresses me with a practical application of the truth to my life.

   ❏ c. He gives me an earnest desire that only grows stronger as I pray.

   ❏ d. He creates circumstances around me that open a door of opportunity.

God always takes the initiative (1*b*). He does not wait to see what we want to do for Him. After He has taken the initiative to come to us, He waits until we respond to Him by adjusting ourselves to Him and making ourselves available to Him. In question 2 all four are ways God may reveal His plan or purpose to you. There are others as well. The last two (*c* and *d*), however, must be carefully watched. A self-centered life will have a tendency to confuse its selfish desire with God's will. Circumstances cannot always be a clear direction for God's leadership either. "Open" and "closed doors" are not always indications of God's directions. In seeking God's direction, check to see if prayer, the Scripture, and circumstances agree in the direction that you sense God is leading you.

Now, you may still be saying, "That all sounds perfectly good, but I need some practical help in learning how to apply these concepts." In every situation God demands that you depend on Him, not a method. The key is not a method but a relationship to God. Let me see if I can help you by telling you about a man who learned to walk with God by prayer and faith.

George Mueller's Walk of Faith

George Mueller was a pastor in England during the nineteenth century. He was concerned that God's people had become very discouraged. They no longer looked for God to do anything unusual. They no longer trusted God to answer prayers. They had so little faith.

George Mueller

God began to lead George to pray. George's prayers were for God to lead him to a work that could only be explained by the people as an act of God. George wanted the people to learn that their God was a faithful, prayer-answering God. He came upon Psalm 81:10 that you read in yesterday's lesson—"Open wide your mouth and I will fill it." God began to lead him in a walk of faith that became an outstanding testimony to all who hear of his story.

When George felt led of God to do some work, he prayed for the resources he needed and told no one of the need. He wanted everyone to know that God had provided for the need only in answer to prayer and faith. During his ministry in Bristol, George started the Scriptural Knowledge Institute for distribution of Scripture and for religious education. He also began an orphanage. By the time of his death, George Mueller had been used by God to build four orphan houses that cared for 2,000 children at a time. Over 10,000 children had been provided for through the orphanages. He distributed over eight million dollars that had been given to him in answer to prayer. When he died at age 93, his worldly possessions were valued at $800.[1]

Here is how George Mueller summed up the way he entered into a "heart" relationship with God and learned to understand God's voice:

- I seek at the beginning to get my heart into such a state that it has no will of its own in regard to a given matter. Nine-tenths of the trouble with people generally is just here. Nine-tenths of the difficulties are overcome when our hearts are ready to do what we know is God's will.
- Having done this, I do not leave the result to feeling or simple impression. If so, I make myself liable to great delusions.
- I seek the Will of the Spirit of God through, or in connection with, the Word of God. The Spirit and the Word must be combined. If I look to the Spirit alone without the Word, I lay myself open to great delusions also. If the Holy Ghost guides us at all, He will do it according to the Scriptures and never contrary to them.
- I take into account providential circumstances. These often plainly indicate God's Will in connection with His Word and Spirit.
- I ask God in prayer to reveal His Will to me aright.
- Thus, (1) through prayer to God, (2) the study of the Word, and (3) reflection, I come to a deliberate judgment according to the best of my ability and knowledge, and if my mind is thus at peace, and continues so after two or three more petitions, I proceed accordingly.

Check the correct answer for each of the following questions.

1. How did Mueller begin in his search for God's will?

- ❏ a. He tried to decide what he wanted to do for God.
- ❏ b. He tried to make sure he had no will of his own.
- ❏ c. He tried to want only God's will.
- ❏ d. Both b and c.

2. What did Mueller say leads to possible delusions or false directions?

    ❏ a. Basing the decision on feelings alone.
    ❏ b. Following the slightest impressions.
    ❏ c. Looking to the Spirit alone for direction.
    ❏ d. All of the above.

3. In which of the following pairs of things did Mueller look for agreement?

    ❏ a. His desires and circumstances.
    ❏ b. The Spirit and the Word.
    ❏ c. The counsel of others and his own desires.
    ❏ d. Circumstances and a sense of peace.

4. What was the final test whereby Mueller came to a judgment about God's will?

    ❏ a. He identified whether the "door" was open or closed.
    ❏ b. He asked a pastor friend what he thought.
    ❏ c. He proceeded with a hunch and watched to see if it worked.
    ❏ d. He used prayer, Bible study, and reflection to find lasting peace about a proposed direction.

Answers are 1-d, 2-d, 3-b, 4-d. I hope this has helped. Don't get discouraged if it still seems vague. We have much more time to work together. Tomorrow I will start by giving you a real-life example of how God works.

Review today's lesson. Pray and ask God to identify one or more statements or Scriptures that He wants you to understand, learn, or practice. Underline them. Then respond to the following:

What was the most meaningful statement or Scripture you read today?

_____

Reword the statement or Scripture into a prayer of response to God.

_____

_____

_____

What does God want you to do in response to today's study?

_____

Practice quoting your Scripture memory verses aloud or write them on separate paper.

SUMMARY STATEMENTS

- God's revelation of His activity is an invitation for me to adjust my life to Him and join in His work.
- "I seek at the beginning to get my heart into such a state that it has no will of its own in regard to a given matter."
- "I do not leave the result to feeling or simple impression."
- "I seek the Will of the Spirit of God through, or in connection with, the Word of God."

GOD SPEAKS TO HIS PEOPLE

God has not changed. He still speaks to His people. God is personal.

Years ago I spoke to a group of young pastors. When I finished the first session, a pastor took me aside and said, "I vowed to God I would never, ever again listen to a man like you. You talk as though God is too personal and real and talks to you. I just despise that."

"Are you having difficulty having God speak to you?" I asked. He and I took time to talk. Before long, we were on our knees. He was weeping and thanking God that God had spoken to him. Oh, don't let anyone intimidate you about hearing from God.

 Read the following Scriptures and answer the questions that follow.

> **Hebrews 1:1–**"In the past God spoke to our forefathers through the prophets at many times and in various ways, but in these last days he has spoken to us by his Son."
>
> **John 14:26–**"The Counselor, the Holy Spirit, whom the Father will send in my name, will teach you all things and will remind you of everything I have said to you."
>
> **John 16:13-14–**"When he, the Spirit of truth, comes, he will guide you into all truth. He will not speak on his own; he will speak only what he hears, and he will tell you what is yet to come. He will bring glory to me by taking from what is mine and making it known to you."
>
> **John 8:47–**"He who belongs to God hears what God says. The reason you do not hear is that you do not belong to God."

1. In the Old Testament ("times past") how did God speak and through whom?

_____

2. In New Testament times ("these last days") how did God speak?

_____

3. In John 14:26 whom did Jesus promise the Father would send in His name?

_____

4. What is the work of the Holy Spirit described in John 14:26 and 16:13-14?

_____

5. Who is the one who hears what God says?

_____

6. What does John 8:47 have to say about a person who does not hear what God says?

_____

Write a summary of what these Scriptures say about God's speaking.

_____

_____

_____

_____

In the Old Testament God spoke in a variety of ways. Through Jesus, God spoke to His people during His time on earth. Now God speaks through the Holy Spirit. The Holy Spirit will teach you all things, will call to your memory the things Jesus said, will guide you into all truth, and will glorify Christ.

Does God really speak to His people in our day? Will He reveal to you where He is working when He wants to use you? Yes! God has not changed. He still speaks to His people.

How Do I Know When God Speaks?

If you have trouble hearing God speak, you are in trouble at the very heart of your Christian experience.

Sin has so affected us (Rom. 3:10-11), you and I cannot understand the truth of God unless the Holy Spirit of God reveals it to us. He is the Teacher. When He teaches you the Word of God, sit before Him and respond to Him. As you pray, watch to see how He uses the Word of God to confirm in your heart a word from God. Watch what He is doing around you in circumstances. The God who is speaking to you as you pray and the God who is speaking to you in the Scriptures is the God who is working around you.

Look on the inside back cover at the fourth reality statement. Then answer the following questions.

1. When Jesus returned to heaven, which Person of the trinity was sent to speak to God's people? Check one.

   ❏ a. God the Father
   ❏ b. Jesus
   ❏ c. The Holy Spirit

2. What are four ways through which He speaks?

   _____

3. When He speaks, what does He reveal?

   _____

God speaks by the Holy Spirit through the Bible, prayer, circumstances, and the church to reveal Himself, His purposes, and His ways. Later in the course, we will study these ways God speaks. I cannot give you a formula, however, and say that this is how you can know when God is speaking to you. I will simply share with you what the Scriptures say.

The key to knowing God's voice is not found in a method you can follow. Knowing God's voice comes from an intimate love relationship with God. That is why those who do not have the relationship ("do not belong to God") do not hear what God is saying (John 8:47). You are going to have to watch to see how God uniquely communicates with you.

Which of the following best describes the way you will know the voice of God when He speaks. Check your response.

   ❏ a. God will give me a miraculous sign. Then I will know God has spoken to me.
   ❏ b. Out of an intimate relationship with God, I will come to recognize God's voice.
   ❏ c. When I learn and follow the correct formula I will hear God speaking.
   ❏ d. I can open the Bible, pick out a verse that I want to use, and claim that I have a word from God for my circumstance.

What is the key to knowing God's voice?_____

The *relationship* is the key to knowing God's voice, to hearing when God speaks. *B* is the correct answer to the preceding question. Now what about *a*, *c*, and *d*? Sometimes in Scripture God did give a miraculous sign to assure the person that the word was from Him. Gideon is one example (Judg. 6). However, asking God for a sign is often an indication of unbelief. When the scribes and Pharisees asked Jesus for a miraculous sign, Jesus condemned them as a "wicked and adulterous generation" (Matt. 12:38-39). They were so self-centered and sinful, they could not even recognize that God was there in their midst (see Luke 19:41-44).

A "correct formula" is not the way either. How many other burning bushes were there like the one Moses experienced? None. God does not want you to become an expert at using a formula.

Some may wonder why answer *d* is not acceptable. They may ask, "Can't I get a word from God from the Bible?" Yes you can! But only the Holy Spirit of God can reveal to you which truth of Scripture is a word from God in a particular circumstance. Notice how self-centered answer *d* is? "*I* open . . . *I* pick . . . *I* claim . . . " Even if the circumstance is similar to yours, only God can reveal His word for your circumstance.

You also need to be very careful about claiming you have a word from God. Claiming to have a word from God is serious business. If you have been given a word from God, you must continue in that direction until it comes to pass (even 25 years like Abram). If you have not been given a word from God—but you say you have—you stand in judgment as a false prophet (see Deut. 18:21-22).

God loves you. He wants you to depend only on Him when you are seeking a word from Him. He wants you to learn to hear His voice and know His will. Your relationship to God is the key to hearing when He speaks to you.

 Consider praying the following prayer: "God, I pray that I will come to such a relationship with You that, when you speak, I will hear and respond."

Review today's lesson. Pray and ask God to identify one or more statements or Scriptures that He wants you to understand, learn, or practice. Underline them. Then respond to the following:

What was the most meaningful statement or Scripture you read today?

_____

Reword the statement or Scripture into a prayer of response to God.

_____

What does God want you to do in response to today's study?

_____

SUMMARY STATEMENTS

- God has not changed. He still speaks to His people.
- If I have trouble hearing God speak, I am in trouble at the very heart of my Christian experience.
- God speaks by the Holy Spirit through the Bible, prayer, circumstances, and the church to reveal Himself, His purposes, and His ways.
- Knowing God's voice comes from an intimate love relationship with God.

GOD SPEAKS WITH A PURPOSE

God develops character to match the assignment.

We usually want God to speak to us so He can give us a devotional thought to make us feel good all day. If you want God to speak to you, you need to be ready for Him to reveal to you what He is doing where you are. In Scripture God is not often seen speaking to people just for conversation's sake. He was always up to something. When God speaks to you through the Bible, prayer, circumstances, the church, or in some other way, He has a purpose in mind for your life.

God Had a Job for Abram

When God spoke to Abram (Gen. 12), what was God about to do? He was about to begin to build a nation. Notice God's timing. Why did God speak to Abram when He did? Because it was then that God wanted to start to build a nation. The moment Abram knew what God was about to do, he had to make an adjustment in his life to God. He had to immediately follow what God said.

The moment God speaks to you is the very moment God wants you to respond to Him.

The moment God speaks to you is the very moment God wants you to respond to Him. Some of us assume that we have the next three to four months to think about it and to try to decide whether this is really God's timing. The moment God speaks to you is God's timing.

How long was it from the time that God spoke to Abram (later named Abraham) that Isaac, the child of promise, was born? Twenty-five years! (See Gen. 12:4 and 21:5.) Why did God wait 25 years? Because it took God 25 years to make a father suitable for Isaac. God was concerned, not so much about Abram, but about a nation. The quality of the father will affect the quality of all the generations that follow. God took time to build Abram into a man of character. Abram had to begin to adjust his life to God's ways immediately. He could not wait until Isaac was born and then try to become the father God wanted him to be.

 Mark the following statements as T (true) or F (false).

____ 1. God speaks to me just so I can have a devotional thought to make me feel good all day.

____ 2. God speaks to me when He has a purpose in mind for my life.

____ 3. When God speaks to me, I can take plenty of time deciding when and how I should respond.

____ 4. When God speaks to me, I must respond immediately by adjusting my life to Him, His purposes, and His ways.

____ 5. The moment God speaks is God's timing.

The moment God speaks to you is God's timing.

When God speaks, He has a purpose in mind for your life. The time He speaks is the time you need to begin responding to Him. False: 1 and 3; True: 2, 4, and 5.

Before we move to our next topic, respond to this: Suppose you had planned to go to a movie or watch a football game or go to the shopping mall. Then God confronts you with an opportunity to join Him in something He wants to do. What would you do? **Check your response:**

❏ 1. I would finish my plans and then fit God's plans into the next available time in my schedule.

❏ 2. I would assume that, since God already knew my plans, this new assignment must not be from Him.

❏ 3. I would try to work out a way to do both what I want and what God wants.

❏ 4. I would adjust my plans to join God in what He was about to do.

Being Available for God's Assignment

I have known some people who would not interrupt a trip to the mall or a football game for anything in the world. In their mind they say they want to serve God, but they keep eliminating from their life anything that is going to interfere with their own plans. They are so self-centered that they do not recognize the times when God comes to them. If you are God-centered, you will adjust your circumstances to what God wants to do.

> God has a right to interrupt your life. He is Lord. When you accepted Him as Lord, you gave Him the right to help Himself to your life anytime He wants.

Suppose that five times out of ten when the Master had something for the servant to do the servant said, "I am sorry. That is not on my schedule." What do you suppose the Master would do? The Master would discipline the servant. If the servant did not respond to the discipline, sooner or later that servant would find that the Master is no longer coming to him with assignments.

You may be saying, "Oh, I wish I could experience God working through me the way John (or Sue) does." But every time God comes to John, John adjusts his life to God and is obedient. When John has been faithful in little assignments, God has given him more important assignments.

If you are not willing to be faithful in a little, God cannot give you a larger assignment. The smaller assignments of God are always used of God to develop character. God always develops character to match His assignment. If God has a great assignment for you, He has to develop a great character to match that assignment before He can give you the assignment.

 Reflect over these matters of lordship and how God develops character for the assignment. Answer the following questions:

1. What kind of assignments have you wanted the Lord to give you? Have you been frustrated or disappointed in this area of your life?

   _____

   _____

2. Can you think of a time when God wanted to use you in an assignment and you chose not to follow His leading? If so, briefly describe the situation.

   _____

   _____

3. Is the Holy Spirit saying anything to you right now about your character? If so, what is He saying?

   _____

4. Do your actions acknowledge Christ as Lord of your life? If not, what response do you want to make to His claims on your life right now?

   _____

   _____

When God tells you a direction, you accept the instruction and understand it clearly; then give God all the time He needs to make you the kind of person He could trust

---

"Well done, good and faithful servant! You have been faithful with a few things; I will put you in charge of many things. Come and share your master's happiness!"
—Matthew 25:21

If you are not willing to be faithful in a little, God cannot give you a larger assignment.

God needs time to prepare you for an assignment.

with that assignment. Do not assume that the moment He calls you you are ready for the assignment.

David How long was it after God (through Samuel) anointed David king that David became king? Maybe 10 or 12 years. What was God doing in the meantime? He was building David's relationship with Himself. As goes the king, so goes the nation. You cannot bypass character.

Paul How long was it after the living Lord called the Apostle Paul that Paul went on his first missionary journey? Maybe 10 or 11 years. The focus is not on Paul; the focus is on God. God wanted to redeem a lost world, and He wanted to begin to redeem the Gentiles through Paul. God needed that much time to prepare Paul for the assignment.

Is it for your sake that God takes time to prepare you? Not for you alone, but also for the sake of those He wants to reach through you. For their sake, give yourself to the kind of relationship to God we are discussing. Then, when He puts you in an assignment, He will achieve everything He wants in the lives of those you touch.

Review today's lesson. Pray and ask God to identify one or more statements or Scriptures that He wants you to understand, learn, or practice. Then respond to the following:

What was the most meaningful statement or Scripture you read today?

_____

Reword the statement or Scripture into a prayer of response to God.

_____

What does God want you to do in response to today's study?

_____

Write your Scripture memory verse (Ps. 20:7) on the following lines.

_____

_____

SUMMARY STATEMENTS

- The moment God speaks to me is the very moment God wants me to respond to Him.
- The moment God speaks to me is God's timing.
- God develops my character to match the assignment He has for me.
- God has a right to interrupt my life. He is Lord. When I accepted Him as Lord, I gave Him the right to help Himself to my life anytime He wants.

---

[1]For further reading on George Mueller see, *Answers to Prayer from George Mueller's Narratives*, Compiled by A. E. C. Brooks, Moody Press; *George Mueller* by Faith Coxe Bailey, Moody Press.

GOD PURSUES A LOVE RELATIONSHIP

CARRIE'S CANCER

When our only daughter Carrie was 16, the doctors told us she had cancer. That meant she would have to go through chemotherapy and radiation. We suffered along with Carrie as we watched her experience the sickness that happens with the treatments. Some people face such an experience by blaming God and questioning why He doesn't love them any more. Carrie's cancer treatments could have been a very devastating experience for our family. Was God loving us still? Yes. Had His love changed? No, His love had not changed.

When you face circumstances like this, you can question and ask God to help you understand what is going on. We did that. We had to ask Him what we should do. We asked all those questions; but I never said, "Lord, I guess you don't love me." With all the pain, I knew He loved us.

At times I went before the Heavenly Father, and I saw behind my daughter the cross of Jesus Christ. I said, "Father, don't ever let me look at circumstances and question your love for me. Your love for me was settled on the cross. That has never changed and will never change for me." Our love relationship with the Heavenly Father sustained us through a very difficult time.

No matter what the circumstances are, God's love never changes. Long before this experience with Carrie, I had made a determination: No matter what the circumstances, I would never look at those circumstances except against the backdrop of the cross. In the death and resurrection of Jesus Christ, God forever convinced me that He loved me. The cross, the death of Jesus Christ, and His resurrection are God's final, total, and complete expression that He loves us.

When bad things happen to you, you may ask "Why?" God understands your questioning. But, as you question, remember that God loves you. Never allow your heart to question the love of God. Settle it on the front end of your desiring to know Him and experience Him that He loves you. He created you for that love relationship. He has been pursuing you in that love relationship. Every dealing He has with you is an expression of His love for you. God would cease to be God if He expressed Himself in any way other than *perfect love!*

Unit

3

Jesus replied: "'Love the Lord your God with all your heart and with all your soul and with all your mind.' This is the first and greatest commandment."

—MATTHEW 22:37-38

Verse to Memorize This Week

CREATED FOR A LOVE RELATIONSHIP

A love relationship with God is more important than any other single factor in your life.

In the first two units I introduced you to some basic principles for knowing and doing the will of God. The seven realities you have examined summarize the kind of relationship through which God works to accomplish His purposes. As I said earlier, this course is not written to teach you a program, a method, or a formula for knowing and doing the will of God. It is written to point you to a *relationship* with God. God will then work through that relationship to accomplish through you what He pleases.

 As a review, see if you can fill in the blanks with the correct words to express the seven realities. If you need help, you may look on the inside back cover of your book.

1. _____ is always at work around you.

2. God pursues a continuing love _____ with you that is real and _____.

3. God invites you to become _____ with Him in His _____.

4. God speaks by the _____ _____ through the Bible, _____, circumstances, and the _____ to reveal Himself, His _____, and His ways.

5. God's invitation for you to work with Him always leads you to a crisis of _____ that requires _____ and action.

6. You must make major _____ in your life to join God in what He is doing.

7. You come to know God by _____ as you _____ Him and He accomplishes His work through you.

This unit will focus on the second reality. Write the second reality below but replace the word *you* with *me*.

_____

_____

Check your work using the inside back cover.

A Love Relationship

During this unit, I want to help you see that God pursues a love relationship with you. He is the One who takes the initiative to bring you into this kind of relationship. He created you for such a relationship. That is the very purpose for your life. This love relationship can and should be real and personal for you.

 If you were standing before God, could you describe your relationship to Him by saying, "I love You with all my heart and all my soul and all my mind and all my strength"? Yes ❑   No ❑   Why?

_____

Can you describe your relationship with God by sincerely saying, "I love You with all of my heart"?

One of our church members was always having difficulty in his personal life, in his family life, at work, and in the church. One day I went to him and asked, "Can you describe your relationship with God by sincerely saying, 'I love You with all of my heart'?"

The strangest look came over his face. "Nobody has ever asked me that," he replied. "No, I could not describe my relationship with God that way. I could say I obey Him, I serve Him, I worship Him, and I fear Him. But I cannot say that I love Him with all my heart."

I realized that everything in the man's life was out of order, because God's basic purpose for his life was out of order. God created us for a love relationship with Him. If you cannot describe your relationship with God by saying that you love Him with all your being, then you need to ask the Holy Spirit to bring you into that kind of relationship.

 If you need to and are willing, pause right now and ask the Holy Spirit to bring you into a whole-hearted love relationship with God.

Spend time in prayer expressing your love to God. Thank Him for the ways He has shown His love to you. Be specific in naming the ways. You may want to list some in the margin. Praise God for His loving-kindness.

The Greatest Commandment

The call to love God with all one's heart is expressed throughout the Old Testament. The essence of the New Testament is the same. Quoting from Deuteronomy, Jesus said the greatest commandment in the law is: "Love the Lord your God with all your heart and with all your soul and with all your mind and with all your strength" (Mark 12:30). Everything depends on this! Everything in your Christian life, everything about knowing and experiencing God, everything about knowing His will, depends on the quality of your love relationship with Him. If that is not right, nothing in your life will be right.

Everything in your Christian life, everything about knowing God and experiencing Him, everything about knowing His will, depends on the quality of your love relationship to God.

 As you read the following Scriptures, emphasize the word *love* (or any form of it, such as "*loves*") by circling the word each time it appears.

> **Deuteronomy 30:19-20**–"This day I call heaven and earth as witnesses against you that I have set before you life and death, blessings and curses. Now choose life, so that you and your children may live and that you may love the Lord your God, listen to his voice, and hold fast to him. For the Lord is your life."

> **John 3:16**–"God so loved the world that he gave his one and only Son, that whoever believes in him shall not perish but have eternal life."

> **John 14:21**–"Whoever has my commands and obeys them, he is the one who loves me. He who loves me will be loved by my Father, and I too will love him and show myself to him."

> **Romans 8:35, 37, 39**–"Who shall separate us from the love of Christ? Shall trouble or hardship or persecution or famine or nakedness or danger or sword? . . . No, in all these things we are more than conquerors through him who loved us. . . . [Nothing] will be able to separate us from the love of God that is in Christ Jesus our Lord."

> **1 John 4:9-10, 19**–"This is how God showed his love among us: He sent his one and only Son into the world that we might live through him. This is love: not that we loved God, but that he loved us and sent his Son as an atoning sacrifice for our sins. . . . We love because he first loved us."

Using the preceding Scriptures, answer the following questions:

1. Who is your "life"?_____

2. In what ways has God demonstrated His love for us?

_____

3. How can we show our love for Him?

_____

4. What does God promise to do in response to our loving Him?

_____

5. Who loved first—we or God?_____

Answers: (1) The Lord is your life. (2) He has drawn us to Himself. He sent His only Son to provide eternal life for us. (3) Choose life; listen to His voice; hold fast to Him; believe in His only Son; obey His commands and teachings. (4) We and our children will live under His blessings. By believing in Jesus, we have eternal life. The Father will love us. God will come to make His home with us. He will make us more than conquerors over all difficulties. We never will be separated from His love. (5) God loved us first. His very nature is love.

A love relationship with God is more important than any other single factor in your life.

What is the one thing God wants from you? He wants you to love Him with all your being. Experiencing God depends on having this relationship of love. A love relationship with God is more important than any other factor in your life.

Review today's lesson. Pray and ask God to identify one or more statements or Scriptures that He wants you to understand, learn, or practice. Underline it (them). Then respond to the following:

What was the most meaningful statement or Scripture you read today?

_____

Reword the statement or Scripture into a prayer of response to God.

_____

What does God want you to do in response to today's study?

_____

Write your Scripture memory verse for this unit in the margin, and review your verses from other units. Remember, you may select a different verse.

On Day 3 you will be given an assignment that may require some advance planning. Turn to page 46 and read "Day 3's Assignment" so you can prepare.

SUMMARY STATEMENTS

- My Christian life depends on the quality of my love relationship with God.
- God created me for a love relationship with Him.
- Everything God says and does is an expression of love.
- A love relationship with God is more important than any other single factor in my life.

A LOVE RELATIONSHIP WITH GOD

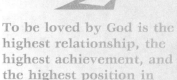
What Would You Honestly Choose?

Picture in your mind a tall ladder leaning against a wall. Now think about your life as a process of climbing that ladder. Wouldn't it be a tragedy to get to the top of the ladder and find you placed it against the wrong wall? One life to live and you missed it!

Earlier in the course we talked about your life being God-centered. That means your life must be properly related to God. This is the love relationship for which you were created—a God-centered love relationship. Your relationship to God (Father, Son, and Spirit) is the single most important aspect of your life. If it is not right, nothing else is important.

 Read the following hymn by George Beverly Shea. Circle all things that may compete with Jesus for a person's love and attention.

> I'd rather have Jesus than silver or gold,
> I'd rather be His than have riches untold;
> I'd rather have Jesus than houses or lands,
> I'd rather be led by His nail-pierced hand.
>
> I'd rather have Jesus than men's applause,
> I'd rather be faithful to His dear cause;
> I'd rather have Jesus than world-wide fame,
> I'd rather be true to His holy name.
>
> He's fairer than lilies of rarest bloom,
> He's sweeter than honey from out the comb;
> He's all that my hungering spirit needs,
> I'd rather have Jesus and let Him lead.[1]

If you could only have one or the other in each of the following pairs, which would you honestly choose? Check your response.

1. I would rather have
   - ❏ Jesus
   - ❏ Silver, gold, riches untold, houses and lands

2. I would rather have
   - ❏ Jesus
   - ❏ People's applause

3. I would rather have
   - ❏ Jesus
   - ❏ World-wide fame

Do you really want to love the Lord your God with all of your heart? He will allow no competitors. He says: "No one can serve two masters. Either he will hate the one and love the other, or he will be devoted to the one and despise the other. You cannot serve both God and Money" (Matt. 6:24).

"You cannot serve both God and Money."

Created Not for Time, but Eternity

God did not create you for time; He created you for eternity. Time (your lifetime on earth) provides the opportunity to get acquainted with Him. It is an opportunity for Him to develop your character in His likeness.

If you just live for time (the here and now), you will miss the ultimate purpose of creation. If you live for time, you will allow your past to mold and shape your life today. Your life as a child of God ought to be shaped by the future (what you will

To be loved by God is the highest relationship, the highest achievement, and the highest position in life.

be one day). God uses your present time to mold and shape your future usefulness here on earth and in eternity.

 What are some of the things in your past that are having a strong limiting influence on your life today? These may include handicaps, a troubled family background, failures, shame over some personal or family "secret" or such things as pride, success, fame, recognition, and possessions.

_____

Do you think you are primarily being shaped by your past or by your future? Why?

_____

Paul struggled with this problem.

Paul struggled with this problem. Here was his approach to dealing with his past and present:

> 4 If anyone else thinks he has reasons to put confidence in the flesh, I have more: 5 circumcised on the eighth day, of the people of Israel, of the tribe of Benjamin, a Hebrew of Hebrews; in regard to the law, a Pharisee; 6 as for zeal, persecuting the church; as for legalistic righteousness, faultless.
>
> 7 But whatever was to my profit I now consider loss for the sake of Christ. 8 What is more, I consider everything a loss compared to the surpassing greatness of knowing Christ Jesus my Lord, for whose sake I have lost all things. I consider them rubbish, that I may gain Christ 9 and be found in him, not having a righteousness of my own that comes from the law, but that which is through faith in Christ—the righteousness that comes from God and is by faith. 10 I want to know Christ and the power of his resurrection and the fellowship of sharing in his sufferings, becoming like him in his death, 11 and so, somehow, to attain to the resurrection from the dead.
>
> 12 Not that I have already obtained all this, or have already been made perfect, but I press on to take hold of that for which Christ Jesus took hold of me. 13 Brothers, I do not consider myself yet to have taken hold of it. But one thing I do: Forgetting what is behind and straining toward what is ahead, 14 I press on toward the goal to win the prize for which God has called me heavenward in Christ Jesus (Phil. 3:4-14).

 Answer the following questions. Read the passage again, if necessary.

1. What are some of the things in Paul's past that could have influenced his present?

_____

2. How did Paul value these things? (v. 8)

_____

3. Why did Paul discredit his past this way? (vv. 8-11)

_____

4. What did Paul do to prepare for a *future* prize? (vv. 13-14)

Forget _____

Strain toward _____

Press on toward _____

Answers: (1) He was faultless in keeping the laws of the Pharisees. He was zealous for God. (2) He considered them as rubbish and loss. (3) Paul wanted to know Christ, be found in Him, and become like Him to attain a *future* blessing (resurrection from the dead). (4) He forgot the past. He looked toward the future. He pressed toward the future goal of a heavenly prize.

Investing in the Future

You need to begin orienting your life to the purposes of God. His purposes go far beyond time and into eternity. Make sure you are investing your life, time, and resources in things that are lasting and not things that will pass away. If you don't recognize that God created you for eternity, you will invest in the wrong direction. You need to store up treasures in heaven. (See Matt. 6:19-21, 33.)

This is why a love relationship with God is so important. He knows what is best for you. Only He can guide you to invest your life in worthwhile ways. This guidance will come as you "walk" with Him and listen to Him.

In what are you investing your life, your time, and your resources? Make two lists below. On the left list things that will pass away. On the right list things that have eternal value.

"Do not store up for yourselves treasures on earth, where moth and rust destroy, and where thieves break in and steal. But store up for yourselves treasures in heaven, where moth and rust do not destroy, and where thieves do not break in and steal. For where your treasure is, there your heart will be also.... But seek first his kingdom and his righteousness, and all these things will be given to you as well."

—Matthew 6:19-21, 33

Think and pray about any adjustments you may need to make in the way you invest your life. Ask God for His perspective on your life. Below write any adjustments you sense God wants you to make.

_____

Review today's lesson. Pray and ask God to identify one or more statements or Scriptures that He wants you to understand, learn, or practice. Underline it (them). Then respond to the following:

What was the most meaningful statement or Scripture you read today?

_____

Reword the statement or Scripture into a prayer of response to God.

_____

What does God want you to do in response to today's study?

_____

SUMMARY STATEMENTS
- To be loved by God is the highest relationship, the highest achievement, and the highest position in life.
- I will let my present be molded and shaped by what I am to become in Christ.
- "Seek first His kingdom and His righteousness."
- I will make sure I am investing in things that are lasting.
- Only God can guide me to invest my life in worthwhile ways.

WALKING WITH GOD

When your relationship is as it ought to be, you will always be in fellowship with the Father.

God created the first man and woman, Adam and Eve, for a love relationship with Himself. After Adam and Eve sinned, they heard God walking in the garden in the "cool of the day." They hid from Him because of their fear and shame. Try to sense the heart of a loving Father when He asked that wonderful love question, "Where are you?" (Gen. 3:9). God knew that something had happened to the love relationship.

Adam and Eve

When your relationship is as it ought to be, you will always be in fellowship with the Father. You will be there in His presence, expecting and anticipating the relationship of love. When Adam and Eve were not there, something had gone wrong.

Quiet Time with God

Early each day, I have an appointment with God. I often wonder what happens when the God who loves me comes to meet me there and I am just not there. How does He feel when He asks, "Henry, where are you?" and there is no answer? I have found this to be true in my own walk with the Lord: I keep that time alone with God, not in order to have a relationship, but because I have a relationship. Because I have that love relationship with the Lord, I want to meet with Him in my quiet time. I want to spend the time there. Time with Him enriches and deepens the relationship I have with Him.

I hear many persons say, "I really struggle trying to have time alone with God." If that is a problem you face, let me suggest something to you. Make the priority in your life to come to love God with all your heart. That will solve most of your problem with your quiet time. You set aside a quiet time because you know Him and therefore love Him, not only to learn about Him. The Apostle Paul said it was "Christ's love" that compelled or constrained him (2 Cor. 5:14).

 Suppose you were dating a person you loved and intended to marry. What is the *primary* reason you date (spend time with) that person? Check only ONE response:

❏ 1. Because I would want to find out about his likes and dislikes.

❏ 2. Because I would want to find out about her family background.

❏ 3. Because I would want to find out about his knowledge and education.

❏ 4. Because I love her and enjoy being with her.

When two people love each other and plan to marry, they are concerned about finding out information about each other. That is not, however, the primary reason why they date. They spend time together because they love each other and enjoy being together.

Similarly, you will learn much about God, His Word, His purposes, and His ways as you spend time with Him. You will come to know Him during the day as you experience Him working in and through your life. Learning about Him is not, however, why you should want to have a quiet time with Him. The more you know Him and experience His love, the more you will love Him. Then you will want that time alone with Him, because you do love Him and enjoy His fellowship.

Day 3's Assignment

Today's lesson is shorter than normal in order to allow time for the following assignment. You may be able to do it today, but you may choose to set aside time later in the week. Plan to complete the assignment sometime prior to your next small-group session. This assignment may require some planning or adapting. Feel free to adjust the assignment to your personal needs and circumstances.

Adam and Eve walked with God in the cool of the day. I want you to set aside at least 30 minutes for a time to "walk with God." If your location, physical condition, and weather permit, find a place outside to walk. Use this time to get out of your routine. You may even want to plan a special trip for part of a day just to be alone with God. The place could be:

___ your neighborhood	___ a wooded area in the country
___ a city park	___ a sandy beach
___ a garden	___ a mountain road
___ a lakeshore	___ anywhere

Spend the time walking and talking with God. If the location permits, you may even want to talk out loud. Focus your thoughts on the love of your Heavenly Father. Praise Him for His love and mercy. Thank Him for expressions of His love to you. Be specific. Express to God your love for Him. Take time to worship Him and adore Him.

After your walk, use the space below to write about your feelings. If they apply, answer some of the following questions:

• How did you feel as you walked and talked with God?
• What aspect of your love relationship with God did you become aware of?
• If this was a difficult or an emotionally uneasy time, why do you think it was?
• What happened that was especially meaningful or joyful?

_____

_____

_____

_____

Practice quoting your Scripture memory verses aloud or write them on a separate piece of paper.

SUMMARY STATEMENTS

• When my relationship is as it ought to be, I will always be in fellowship with the Father.
• I will make the priority in my life to come to love Him with all my heart.
• I will have my quiet time because I know God and love Him, not in order to learn about Him.

GOD PURSUES A LOVE RELATIONSHIP

God takes the initiative. He chooses us, loves us, and reveals His eternal purposes for our lives.

No One Seeks God on His Own Initiative

God always takes the "first step" in this love relationship. God must take the initiative and come to us if we are to experience Him. This is the witness of the entire Bible. He came to Adam and Eve in the garden. In love He fellowshipped with them, and they with Him. He came to Noah, Abraham, Moses, and the prophets. God took the initiative for each person in the Old Testament to experience Him in a personal fellowship of love. This is true of the New Testament as well. Jesus came to the disciples and chose them to be with Him and experience His Love. He came to Paul on the Damascus Road. In our natural human state, we do not seek God on our own initiative.

"There is no one righteous, not even one; there is no one who understands, no one who seeks God. All have turned away, they have together become worthless; there is no one who does good, not even one."
—Romans 3:10-12

 Read Romans 3:10-12 (left) and answer the following questions.

1. How many people are righteous on their own? _____

2. How many people understand spiritual things on their own? _____

3. How many people seek after God on their own? _____

4. How many people do good on their own? _____

No one; not even one! Sin has affected us so deeply that no one seeks after God on his own initiative. Therefore, if we are to have any relationship with Him or His Son, God will have to take the initiative. This is exactly what He does.

God Draws Us to Himself

"No one can come to me [Jesus] unless the Father who sent me draws him. . . . Everyone who listens to the Father and learns from him comes to me. . . . This is why I told you that no one can come to me unless the Father has enabled him."
—John 6:44,45,65

 Read the Scripture on the left and answer the following questions:

1. Who can come to Jesus without being drawn by the Father? _____

2. What does a person do who listens to the Father and learns from Him?

_____

3. What is the only way a person can come to Jesus?

_____

Jeremiah 31:3–"The Lord appeared to us in the past, saying: 'I have loved you with an everlasting love; I have drawn you with loving-kindness.'"

Hosea 11:4–"I led them with cords of human kindness, with ties of love; I lifted the yoke from their neck and bent down to feed them."

The love that God focuses on your life is an everlasting love. Because of that love, He has drawn you to Himself. He has drawn you with cords of love when you were not His friend, when you were His enemy. He gave His own Son to die for you. To firmly anchor the experiencing of God and knowing His will, you must be absolutely convinced of God's love for you.

 How do you know God loves you? What are some reasons you are convinced that God loves you?

_____

_____

God came to Saul, known later as Paul (Acts 9:1-19). Saul was actually opposing God and His activities and fighting against God's Son, Jesus. Jesus came to Paul and revealed the Father's purposes of love for him. This also is true in our lives. We do not choose Him. He chooses us, loves us, and reveals His eternal purposes for our lives.

Jesus said to His disciples: "You did not choose me, but I chose you and appointed you. . . . As it is, you do not belong to the world, but I have chosen you out of the world" (John 15:16, 19). Didn't Peter choose to follow Jesus? No. Jesus chose Peter. Peter responded to the invitation of God. God took the initiative.

Jesus asked the disciples who people said He was. Then He asked them who they thought He was. Peter answered correctly, "You are the Christ." Then Jesus made a very significant statement to Peter, "This was not revealed to you by man, but by my Father in heaven." Peter was responding to God's initiative in his life (Matt. 16:13-17).

 Who had revealed to Peter that Jesus was the Christ, the promised Messiah?

_____

In essence Jesus was saying, "Peter, you could never have known and confessed that I am the Christ unless My Father had been at work in you. He caused you to know who I am. You are responding to the Father's activity in your life. Good!"

Do you realize that God determined to love you? Apart from that you never would have become a Christian. He had something in mind when He called you. He began to work in your life. You began to experience a love relationship with God in which He took the initiative. He began to open your understanding. He drew you to Himself.

 What did you do? Check your response.

❏ 1. I responded to His invitation to a love relationship.
❏ 2. I rejected His offer of a love relationship.

When you responded to His invitation, He brought you into a love relationship with Himself. But you would never know that love, be in the presence of that love, or be aware of that love if God had not taken the initiative.

> You cannot know the activity of God unless
> He takes the initiative to reveal it to you.

 Number the following items from 1 to 4 in the order they occur in the development of a love relationship with God.

_____ a. God comes into my life and fellowships with me.

_____ b. I respond to God's activity in my life and invite Him to do in my life what He pleases.

_____ c. God shows me His love and reveals Himself to me.

_____ d. God chooses me because of His love.

Some of these actions almost seem to happen at the same time. Yet, we can be sure of this—God takes the initiative; then we respond. I numbered the items a-4, b-3, c-2, and d-1. God *always* takes the initiative in loving us.

"When Jesus came to the region of Caesarea Philippi, he asked his disciples, 'Who do people say the Son of Man is?'

"They replied, 'Some say John the Baptist; others say Elijah; and still others, Jeremiah or one of the prophets.'

"'But what about you?' he asked. 'Who do you say I am?'

"Simon Peter answered, 'You are the Christ, the Son of the living God.'

"Jesus replied, 'Blessed are you, Simon son of Jonah, for this was not revealed to you by man, but by my Father in heaven.'"

—Matthew 16:13-17

The following Scriptures speak of God's initiative in the love relationship. Read each passage. Then write a brief summary statement about how God acts (acted) or what He does (did) to take the initiative.

Deuteronomy 30:6–"The Lord your God will give you and your descendants obedient hearts, so that you will love him with all your heart, and you will continue to live in that land" (GNB).

_____

Luke 10:22–"All things have been committed to me by my Father. No one knows who the Son is except the Father, and no one knows who the Father is except the Son and those to whom the Son chooses to reveal him."

_____

John 15:16–"You did not choose me, but I chose you and appointed you to go and bear fruit—fruit that will last."

_____

Philippians 2:13–"It is God who works in you to will and to act according to his good purpose."

_____

1 John 3:16–"This is how we know what love is: Jesus Christ laid down his life for us."

_____

Revelation 3:20–"Here I am! I stand at the door and knock. If anyone hears my voice and opens the door, I will come in and eat with him, and he with me."

_____

Write one of these words in the blank to make the following statement true: never, sometimes, frequently, always.

God _____ takes the initiative to establish a love relationship with me.

Review today's lesson. Pray and ask God to identify one or more statements or Scriptures that He wants you to understand, learn, or practice. Underline it (them). Then respond to the following:

What was the most meaningful statement or Scripture you read today?

_____

Reword the statement or Scripture into a prayer of response to God.

_____

What does God want you to do in response to today's study?

_____

SUMMARY STATEMENTS

- In this love relationship, God always takes the initiative.
- I do not choose Him. He chooses me, loves me, and reveals His eternal purposes for my life.
- I cannot know the activity of God unless He takes the initiative to let me know.

A REAL, PERSONAL, PRACTICAL RELATIONSHIP

The Scriptures Testify of this Relationship

God's plan for the advancement of His kingdom depends on His relationship to His people.

The relationship God wants to have with you will be real and personal. Some ask the question; "Can a person actually have a real, personal, and practical relationship with God?" They seem to think that God is far off and unconcerned about their day-to-day living. That is not the God we see in the Scriptures.

Read one Scripture passage. Then describe at least one fact that indicates the relationship the person(s) had with God was real, personal, and/or practical. If you are already familiar with the story, you may answer from your present knowledge of the passage. Then do the same for the next passage. I have completed the first as an example.

Adam and Eve after they sinned—Genesis 3:20-21 _____

God made clothes for them.

Hagar when she fled from Sarai—Genesis 16:1-13 _____

_____

Solomon and his request for an understanding heart—1 Kings 3:5-13; 4:29-30

_____

The Twelve that Jesus sent out to preach—Mark 6:7-13 _____

_____

Peter in prison awaiting trial—Acts 12:1-17 _____

_____

John on the island of Patmos—Revelation 1:9-20 _____

_____

From Genesis to Revelation, we see God relating to people in real, personal, intimate, and practical ways. God had intimate fellowship with Adam and Eve, walking in the garden with them in the cool of the day. When they sinned, God came after them to restore the love relationship. He met a very practical need by providing clothing to cover their nakedness.

Hagar was used, mistreated, and abused by Sarai. She fled for her life. When she reached the end of her own resources, when she had no where else to turn, when all hope was gone, God came to her. In her relationship with God, she learned that God saw her, knew her needs, and would lovingly provide for her. God is very personal.

Solomon's father, David, had been a man who sought the Lord with his whole heart. Solomon had a heritage of faith and obedience to follow. He had the opportunity to ask and receive anything he wanted from God. Solomon demonstrated his love for God's people by asking for a discerning heart. God granted his request and gave him wealth and fame as well. Solomon found his relationship with God to be very practical.

The disciples also had a real, personal, and practical relationship with Jesus—the Son of God. Jesus had chosen them to be with Him. What a pleasure it must

Adam and Eve

Hagar

Solomon

The Twelve

have been to have such an intimate relationship with Jesus! When they were given a very difficult assignment, Jesus did not send them out helpless. He gave them authority over evil spirits.

Peter

In some places of the world obedience to the Lord results in imprisonment. This was Peter's experience. In answer to prayer, the Lord miraculously delivered him. This was so dramatic and practical that Peter first thought it was a dream. The praying Christians thought he was an angel. Soon, they all discovered that the Lord's deliverance was real. That deliverance probably saved Peter's life.

John

In exile on the island of Patmos, John was spending the Lord's Day in fellowship with God. During this time of fellowship in the Spirit, the revelation of Jesus Christ came to John to "show his servants what must soon take place" (Rev. 1:1). This message has been a genuine challenge and encouragement to the churches from John's day to the present time.

Do you sense, as you read the Scripture, that God became real and personal to people? Do you sense that their relationship with God was practical? Was He also real and personal to Noah? to Abraham? to Moses? to Isaiah? Yes! Yes! Yes! Has God changed? No! This was true in the Old Testament. It was true during the time of Jesus' life and ministry. It was true after the coming of the Holy Spirit at Pentecost. Your life also can reflect that kind of real, personal, and practical relationship as you respond to God's working in your life.

 Briefly describe an experience in your own life when God was real, personal, and/or practical in His relationship to you.

_____

_____

_____

Love must be real and personal. A person cannot love without another "someone" to love. A love relationship with God takes place between two real beings. A relationship with God is real and personal. This has always been His desire. All His efforts are made to bring this desire to reality. God is a Person pouring His life into yours.

If, for some reason, you cannot think of a time when your relationship to God has been real, personal, and practical, you need to spend some time evaluating your relationship with Him. Go before the Lord in prayer and ask Him to reveal the true nature of your relationship with Him. Ask Him to bring you into that kind of relationship. If you come to the realization that you have never entered a saving relationship with God, turn to the activity in Day 1 of Unit 1 (p. 7). for help in settling that most important issue now.

God's Presence and Work in Your Life Is Practical

God is practical.

Some people say to me, "Henry, what you are suggesting about doing God's will is not practical in our day." I always have to differ with them. God is very practical. He was in Scripture. He is the same today. When He provided manna, quail, and water for the children of Israel, He was being practical. When Jesus fed five thousand, He was being practical. The God I see revealed in Scripture is real, personal, and practical. I just trust God to be practical and real to me, too.

The constant presence of God is the most practical part of your life and ministry.

The constant presence of God is the most practical part of your life and ministry. Unfortunately, we often assign God to a limited place in our lives. Then we call on Him whenever we need help. That is the exact opposite of what we find in the

Word of God. He is the One who is working in our world. He invites you to relate to Him, so He can accomplish His work through you. His whole plan for the advance of the Kingdom depends on His working in real and practical ways through His relationship to His people.

Knowing and experiencing God through a real and personal relationship was practical in the Scriptures. I believe you will find that this kind of walk with God is still exceedingly practical. God can make a practical difference in your relationships in your family, in your church, and with other people. You can encounter God in such a way that you know you are experiencing Him.

 Can you describe your relationship with God as real, personal, and practical? Why?

_____

_____

Fill in the blanks to complete the second reality of experiencing God. Make the statement personal.

1. God is always at work around me.

2. God _____ a continuing love _____

with _____ that is _____ and _____.

Review today's lesson. Pray and ask God to identify one or more statements or Scriptures that He wants you to understand, learn, or practice. Underline it (them). Then respond to the following:

What was the most meaningful statement or Scripture you read today?

_____

Reword the statement or Scripture into a prayer of response to God.

_____

_____

What does God want you to do in response to today's study?

_____

Review your Scripture memory verses and be prepared to recite them to a partner in your small-group session this week.

If you have not taken time to "walk with God" and write about the experience on Day 3, try to do so before your small-group session this week.

SUMMARY STATEMENTS

- The relationship God wants to have with me will be real and personal.
- God's whole plan for the advance of the Kingdom depends on His working in real and practical ways through His personal relationship with His people.

LOVE AND GOD'S INVITATION

Unit

4

"RIPE UNTO HARVEST"

Jerry and Cliff had been schoolmates since the sixth grade. But only recently did Jerry realize that Cliff was not a Christian. On several occasions, he had talked to Cliff about the youth activities at church and had invited him to attend some of them. One time he gave Cliff a tract. Cliff's reaction to that was distant, to say the least. "Yeah," he responded, "I know I need to get my life right, but I'll do it later." Not wanting to be pushy, Jerry didn't bring up the subject anymore. But he did find other ways to witness to Cliff, such as being a good friend and living like a Christian.

On a Friday night, Cliff, Jerry, and several friends went bowling. A group of youth from their school were hanging out there and partying. When Cliff and Jerry's group got in the car to leave, Cliff made a comment about how that group of guys in the bowling alley needed to change their lives. To Jerry's surprise, Cliff asked if they would pray for them. So, Jerry pulled the car into a parking lot, and they prayed right there. Then, as they moved on down the road, Cliff began to talk about how he needed to change his life by beginning to go to church and get his life right with God.

Cliff's request and remarks should have signaled to Jerry that Cliff was what the Bible refers to as "ripe unto harvest." But Jerry was a little dense. He thought he was just supposed to plant the seed. Then he would bring Cliff to church and, after a period of time, the youth minister would lead him to Christ. He never expected to have that privilege and responsibility himself. Actually, Cliff practically had to ask Jerry, "Hey, would you tell me what I have to do to be saved?" Nervous and unsure of himself, Jerry introduced Cliff to Jesus, and Cliff accepted Him as Savior and Lord, right there in the car on the way home.

Later, Cliff said that he felt like he had been on a sort of highway for a long time. God had offered him lots of off ramps that would lead to the right road. Each time, he found a reason not to go in that direction. Finally, he took the off ramp that God pointed him to through Jerry.

As a result of the experience in leading Cliff to Christ, Jerry has made a commitment to be more alert to opportunities that God opens up for him to be involved with God in His work.

In this love relationship with God, God's revelation is your invitation to join Him in what He is doing.

Verse to Memorize This Week

Whoever has my commands and obeys them, he is the one who loves me. He who loves me will be loved by my Father, and I too will love him and show myself to him.

—JOHN 14:21

KNOW GOD

This unit continues our focus on the love relationship with God. You will find that the call to relationship is also a call to be on mission with Him. If you want to know God's will, you must respond to His invitation to love Him wholeheartedly. God works through those He loves to carry out His kingdom purposes in the world. During this unit, we will begin to look at how God invites you to become involved with Him in His work.

Knowing God by Experience

You will never be satisfied to just know *about* God. Knowing God only comes through experience as He reveals Himself to you. When Moses was at the burning bush, he asked God, "Suppose I go to the Israelites and say to them, 'The God of your fathers has sent me to you,' and they ask me, 'What is his name?' Then what shall I tell them?" (Ex. 3:13).

God responded, "I AM WHO I AM. This is what you are to say to the Israelites: 'I AM has sent me to you'" (Ex. 3:14). When God said, "I AM WHO I AM" He was saying, "I am the Eternal One. I am everything you will need." During the next 40 years, Moses came to know God experientially as Jehovah or Yahweh, the Great I AM.

I AM WHO I AM

Names of God

The Bible reveals that God has always taken the "first step" to make Himself known through experience. Frequently when God revealed Himself to a person, the person gave God a new name or described Him in a new way. For the Hebrew, a person's name represented his character or described his nature. This is why we frequently see new names or titles for God following an event in which a Bible character experienced God.

Biblical names, titles, and descriptions of God identify how Bible characters personally came to know God. For example: Joshua and the Israelites were fighting the Amalekites. Moses was overseeing the battle from a nearby mountain. While he held his hands up to God, the Israelites were victorious. When he let his hands down they began to lose. God defeated the Amalekites through Israel that day. To celebrate the victory, Moses built an altar and gave it the name "The Lord is my Banner."

The Lord Is My Banner

A banner is the standard that goes out in front of an army to indicate who it represents. "The Lord is my Banner" says we are God's people; He is our God. Moses' uplifted hands gave constant glory to God indicating that the battle was His, and Israel was His. Israel came to know God in a better way as they realized anew: We are God's people; the Lord is our Banner (see Ex. 17:8-15).

For another example read Genesis 22:1-18 and answer these questions:

1. What did God ask Abraham to do? (v. 2)_____

2. What do you think verse 8 indicates about Abraham?_____

3. What did God do for Abraham? (v. 13)_____

4. What name did Abraham give the place? (v. 14)_____

5. Why did God promise to bless Abraham? (vv. 15-18)

_____

God was in the process of developing Abraham's character to be the father of a nation. He put Abraham's faith and obedience to the test. This brought Abraham to a crisis of belief. Abraham had faith that the Lord would provide (v. 8). He made the adjustment of his life to act on his belief that God was Provider. He obeyed God. When God provided a ram, Abraham came to an intimate knowledge of God through the experience of God as his Provider.

 Look at the seven realities on the inside back cover of this book. How does Abraham's experience with God follow that sequence?

_____

Provider of Partners

As a pastor of college students, I called the students in and talked with them regularly. I knew they were in a period of rapid change. I wanted to help them as they made major decisions in their lives. A wonderful girl who was studying nursing came to my office. I had been praying for Sherri and what God might be doing in her life. We talked about her alcoholic father. We talked about her decision of whether or not to continue in nursing. Then I looked at Sherri and said, "Sherri, I want you to know that God has laid on my heart that I need to pray for a husband for you."

She asked, "Are you serious?"

I said, "Sherri, I want you to know I *am* serious. Because you have had an alcoholic father and have experienced all the turmoil and heartache that you have, I believe God wants to give you a wonderful man to love you for who you are. I want you to know that, beginning today, I am praying that God will give you a wonderful, loving husband."

She wept. She and I began to pray that God would provide her a partner. About three months later, God brought into our church a wonderful young man who was an engineering student. They fell in love, and I performed their wedding ceremony. They now have two children and are faithfully serving the Lord. The last I heard, Sherri was as happy as could be.

How did Sherri know that God could provide a husband? She claimed who God was and then proceeded to watch and pray. She was open to receive the one God would give her. She had to obey and receive when God revealed His choice to her. Then she came to know God as the Provider of Partners.

 Describe an event through which you experienced God at work in your life.

_____

What name could you use to describe the God you experienced?

_____

Read the following list of names, titles, and descriptions of God. Circle those that describe God in ways you have personally experienced Him.

my defender (Job 16:19)	bread of life (John 6:35)
Comforter in sorrow (Jer. 8:18)	my confidence (Ps. 71:5)
Wonderful Counselor (Isa. 9:6)	defender of widows (Ps. 68:5)
my strong deliverer (Ps. 140:7)	Faithful and True (Rev. 19:11)
our Father (Isa. 64:8)	a consuming fire (Deut. 4:24)
a sure foundation (Isa. 28:16)	my friend (Job 16:20)
God Almighty (Gen. 17:1)	God of all comfort (2 Cor. 1:3)
God who avenges me (Ps. 18:47)	God who saves me (Ps. 51:14)

our guide (Ps. 48:14)	head of the church (Eph. 5:23)
our Help (Ps. 33:20)	my hiding place (Ps. 32:7)
a great high priest (Heb. 4:14)	Holy One among you (Hos. 11:9)
my hope (Ps. 71:5)	Jealous (Ex. 34:14)
righteous Judge (2 Tim. 4:8)	King of kings (1 Tim. 6:15)
our leader (2 Chron. 13:12)	your life (Col. 3:4)
light of life (John 8:12)	Lord of lords (1 Tim. 6:15)
Lord of the harvest (Matt. 9:38)	mediator (1 Tim. 2:5)
the most holy (Dan. 9:24)	our peace (Eph. 2:14)
Prince of Peace (Isa. 9:6)	my Redeemer (Ps. 19:14)
refuge and strength (Ps. 46:1)	my salvation (Ex. 15:2)
my Savior (Ps. 42:5)	the good shepherd (John 10:11)
Sovereign Lord (Luke 2:29)	my stronghold (Ps. 18:2)
my support (2 Sam. 22:19)	good teacher (Mark 10:17)

As time permits, make brief notes (in the margin) of a few experiences through which you have come to know God in these ways.

Did you see that you have come to know God through experience? Could you circle any of the names and not think of an experience when God acted in that way? For instance, you could not have known God as the "Comforter in sorrow" unless you had *experienced* His comfort during a time of sorrow. You come to know God when He reveals Himself to you. You come to know Him as you experience Him. That is why we have titled this course "Experiencing God."

 How do you come to know God personally and intimately?

_____

You come to know God more intimately as He reveals Himself to you through your experiences with Him.

 Review today's lesson. Pray and ask God to identify one or more statements or Scriptures that He wants you to understand, learn, or practice. Underline it (them). Then respond to the following:

What was the most meaningful statement or Scripture you read today?

_____

Reword the statement or Scripture into a prayer of response to God.

_____

What does God want you to do in response to today's study?

_____

Write your Scripture memory verse for this unit on the following lines and review your verses from other units.

_____

_____

SUMMARY STATEMENTS

- Knowing God only comes through experience as He reveals Himself to me.
- I know God more intimately as He reveals Himself to me through my experiences with Him.

WORSHIP GOD

"O Lord, our Lord, how majestic is your name in all the earth!" (Ps. 8:1).

Yesterday you learned that you come to know God by experience at His initiative ("first step"). You learned that a Hebrew name described a person's character or nature. The name was closely associated with the person and his presence. Thus, to call on one's name was to seek the presence of that person. God's name is majestic and worthy of our praise. Acknowledging God's name amounts to recognizing God for who He is. Calling on His name indicates you are seeking His presence. Praising His name is praising *Him*. God's names in Scripture can become a call to worship for you.

Spend this day in worship of God through His names. To focus your attention on His name is to focus attention on the God of the name. His name represents His presence. To worship God is to reverence and honor Him, to acknowledge Him as worthy of your praise. The Psalms are rich in their instructions to direct your worship toward God through His name.

 Read the following Scriptures and circle or underline the word or phrase in each verse that describes a way you can direct your worship toward God through His names.

"Sing unto the Lord, bless his name" (Ps. 96:2, KJV).

"Revive us, and we will call on your name" (Ps. 80:18).

"I will declare your name to my brothers" (Ps. 22:22).

"Give me an undivided heart, that I may fear your name" (Ps. 86:11).

"Save us, O Lord our God, and gather us from the nations, that we may give thanks to your holy name and glory in your praise" (Ps. 106:47).

"All the nations you have made will come and worship before you, O Lord; they will bring glory to your name" (Ps. 86:9).

"Glory in his holy name; let the hearts of those who seek the Lord rejoice" (Ps. 105:3).

"I will praise you forever for what you have done; in your name I will hope, for your name is good" (Ps. 52:9).

"Those who know your name will trust in you, for you, Lord, have never forsaken those who seek you" (Ps. 9:10).

"In him our hearts rejoice, for we trust in his holy name" (Ps. 33:21).

"Thus will I bless thee while I live: I will lift up my hands in thy name" (Ps. 63:4, KJV).

"Let all who take refuge in you be glad; let them ever sing for joy. Spread your protection over them, that those who love your name may rejoice in you" (Ps. 5:11).

"In God we make our boast all day long, and we will praise your name forever" (Ps. 44:8).

"Blessed are those who have learned to acclaim you, who walk in the light of your presence, O Lord. They rejoice in your name all day long; they exult in your righteousness" (Ps. 89:15-16).

"In the night I remember your name, O Lord, and I will keep your law" (Ps. 119:55).

"Cover their faces with shame so that men will seek your name, O Lord" (Ps. 83:16).

"I will give thanks to the Lord because of his righteousness and will sing praise to the name of the Lord Most High" (Ps. 7:17).

"All the earth bows down to you; they sing praise to you, they sing praise to your name" (Ps. 66:4).

WAYS TO WORSHIP GOD

bless *His name*
call upon *His name*
declare *His name*
fear *His name*
give thanks to *His name*

glorify *His name*
glory in *His name*
hope in *His name*
know *His name*
lift up hands in *His name*
love *His name*
praise *His name*
rejoice in *His name*

remember *the name*
seek *His name*
sing praise to *His name*
sing to *His name*
trust in *His name*

 Use these ways to worship God right now. Turn to "Names, Titles, and Descriptions of God" (p. 157). Spend the remainder of your study time today in worship. The names direct your attention to God, who He is, and what He does. Praise Him for who He is. Thank Him for what He has done. Glorify Him. Love and adore Him.

Seek Him. Trust Him. Sing to Him. Take as much time as you like for this period of worship. Make this a meaningful time to experience your love relationship with the Lord.

Briefly summarize what you thought, felt, or experienced during this time of worship. What was the most meaningful part of this time of worship?

_____

_____

_____

LOVE GOD

*"Whoever has my commands
and obeys them, he is the one
who loves me. He who loves
me will be loved by my Father,
and I too will love him and
show myself to him."*
—*John 14:21*

Love?

Obey!

God takes the initiative to pursue a love relationship with you. This love relationship, however, is not one-sided. He wants you to know Him and worship Him. Most of all, He wants you to love Him.

 Read this unit's suggested memory verse in the left margin and answer these questions.

1. Who is the one who loves Jesus? _____

2. How does the Father respond to the one who loves Jesus? _____

3. What will Jesus do for the one who loves Him? _____

Jesus said, "If you love me, you will obey what I command" (John 14:15). When you obey Jesus, you show that you love and trust Him. The Father loves those who love His Son. Obedience is the outward expression of your love of God.

Jesus set an example of love for you in His life. He said, "The world must learn that I love the Father and that I do exactly what my Father has commanded me" (John 14:31). Jesus was obedient to every command of the Father. He demonstrated His love for the Father by obedience. The reward for obedience and love is that He will show Himself to you.

 How can you demonstrate your love for God?

_____

A love relationship with God requires that you demonstrate your love by obedience. This is not just a following of the "letter" of the law; it is a following of the "spirit" of the command as well. If you have an obedience problem, you have a love problem.

God's Nature

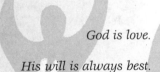

God is love.

His will is always best.

God's nature is love. He will always express His will toward you in perfect love. He never gives you second best. He will bring discipline, judgment, and wrath on those who continue in sin and rebellion. His disciplines, however, are always based on love (Heb. 12:6). Two verses describe His love toward us:
• John 3:16—"God so loved the world that he gave his one and only Son."
• 1 John 3:16—"This is how we know what love is: Jesus Christ laid down his life for us."

 Read 1 John 4:16. Then fill in the two blanks in the statements below.

God is _____. His will is always _____.

Your relationship with God reveals what you believe about Him. It is spiritually impossible for you to believe one way and practice another. If you really believe that God is *love*, you will also accept the fact that His will is always best.

*God is all-knowing.
His directions are
always right.*

By nature God is omniscient—all-knowing. He has all knowledge—past, present, and future. Nothing is outside the knowledge of God. Whenever God expresses Himself to you, therefore, His directions are always right.

 Fill in the two blanks in the statements below.

God is all _____. His directions are always _____

You never have to question whether God's will is best or right. It always is best and right. This is true because He loves you and knows everything. Because He loves you perfectly, you can trust Him and obey Him completely.

God is omnipotent—all-powerful. He can accomplish anything He purposes to do. If He ever asks you to do something, He Himself will enable you to do it. We will look at this fact more closely during Day 5.

 Fill in the two blanks in the statements below.

God is all _____. He can _____ me to do His will.

Match the fact about the nature of God on the left with the correct statement of application on the right. Write the correct letters in the blanks.

_____ 1. God is love.
_____ 2. God is all-knowing.
_____ 3. God is all-powerful.

a. God's directions are right.
b. God can enable me to do His will.
c. God's will is best.

When your life is in the middle of God's activity, He will start rearranging a lot of your thinking. God's ways and thoughts are so different from yours and mine that they often will sound wrong or crazy. You need a readiness to believe God and trust Him completely. You need to believe that what He is doing is best for you. Don't try to second-guess God. Just let Him be God. Answers are: 1-c; 2-a; 3-b.

God will start to make Himself known to you very simply as He would to a child. As you respond to Him with simple childlike trust, a whole new way of looking at life will begin to unfold for you. Your life will be fulfilling. When you have God, you have everything there is.

 When you hear words like *commands, judgments, statutes, or laws,* is your first impression negative or positive? Negative ❑ Positive ❑

God's Commands

God's commands are expressions of His nature of love. In Deuteronomy 10:12-13 He said the commands are for our own good:

> What does the Lord your God ask of you but to fear the Lord your God, to walk in all his ways, to love him, to serve the Lord your God with all your heart and with all your soul, and to observe the Lord's commands and decrees that I am giving you today for your own good?

 Read Deuteronomy 32:46-47 in the margin. How important are God's words to you?

_____

The foundation of these passages is the love relationship. When you come to know God by experience, you will be convinced of His love. When you are convinced of His love you can believe Him and trust Him. When you love and trust Him, you can obey Him. "This is love for God: to obey his commands. And his commands are not burdensome" (1 John 5:3).

Suppose you had to cross a field full of land mines. A person who knew exactly where each one was buried offered to take you through the field. Would you say to him, "I don't want you to tell me what to do. I don't want you to impose your ways on me"? I don't know about you, but I would stay as close to that person as

God is all-powerful. He can enable you to do His will.

"He said to them, 'Take to heart all the words I have solemnly declared to you this day, so that you may command your children to obey carefully all the words of this law. They are not just idle words for you—they are your life. By them you will live long in the land you are crossing the Jordan to possess.'"
—Deuteronomy 32:46-47

"In the future, when your son asks you, 'What is the meaning of the stipulations, decrees and laws the Lord our God has commanded you?' tell him. . . . 'The Lord commanded us to obey all these decrees and to fear the Lord our God, so that we might always prosper and be kept alive, as is the case today. And if we are careful to obey all this law before the Lord our God, as he has commanded us, that will be our righteousness.'"
—Deuteronomy 6:20-25

I could. I certainly would not go wandering off. His directions to me would be to preserve my life. He would say, "Don't go that way, because that way will kill you. Go this way, and you will live."

Life has some land mines that can destroy you or wreck your life. Because God loves you, He does not want to see your life wrecked. So, He has given you guidelines for living. He wants you to have life and have it abundantly. When the Lord gives you a command, He is trying to protect and preserve the best He has for you. He does not want you to lose it.

 Read Deuteronomy 6:20-25 in the margin and answer the following questions.

What is the purpose of God's commands? _____

What are some "land mines" you face in your life?

_____

How can God's commands help you deal with these problems?

_____

Know Him

Love Him

Believe Him

Trust Him

Obey Him

So you may prosper and live life to its fullest measure.

God's commands are designed to guide you to life's very best. You will not obey Him, however, if you do not believe Him and trust Him. You cannot believe Him, if you do not love Him. You cannot love Him, unless you know Him.

If you really come to know God as He reveals Himself to you, you will love Him. If you love Him, You will believe and trust Him. If you believe and trust Him, you will obey Him.

God is love. Because of His love, His will for you is always best. He is all knowing; so His directions are always right. He has given His commands so that you may prosper and live life to its fullest measure.

Review today's lesson. Pray and ask God to identify one or more statements or Scriptures that He wants you to understand, learn, or practice. Underline it (them). Then respond to the following:

What was the most meaningful statement or Scripture you read today?

_____

Reword the statement or Scripture into a prayer of response to God.

_____

What does God want you to do in response to today's study?

_____

SUMMARY STATEMENTS

- Obedience is the outward expression of my love of God.
- If I have an obedience problem, I have a love problem.
- God is love. His will is always best.
- God is all-knowing. His directions are always right.
- God is all-powerful. He can enable me to do His will.
- All of God's commands are expressions of His nature of love.
- When God gives a commandment, He is not restricting me. He is freeing me.
- If I love Him, I will obey Him!

GOD INVITES YOU TO JOIN HIM

When you see the Father at work around you, that is your invitation to adjust your life to Him and join Him in that work.

The Bible is the record of God's activity in the world. It is not primarily a book about individual persons and their relationship with God (Abraham, Moses, or Paul), but rather the activity of God and His relationship with individuals. The focus is on God and His activity.

 Review the first four realities we have been looking at in this course. Fill in the blanks below with the correct words. If you need help, look on the inside back cover.

1. _____ is always at work around you.

2. God _____ a continuing love _____ with you that is real and _____.

3. God invites you to become _____ with Him in His _____.

4. God speaks by the _____ _____ through the Bible, _____, circumstances, and the _____ to reveal Himself, His _____, and His ways.

God Works Through People

The Bible reveals that God always has been involved in the world. As we read the Bible, we are reading about the saving activity of God in our world. We see that He chooses to take the initiative and involve His people in His work. He chooses to work *through* His people to accomplish His purposes.

God is at work in the world.

When God was ready to judge the world, He came to Noah. He was about to do something, and He was going to do it through Noah. When God was ready to build a nation for Himself, He came to Abraham. God was going to accomplish His will through Abraham. When God decided to deliver the children of Israel, He appeared to Moses. He planned to deliver Israel through Moses.

The fact that God involves His people in His work is evident all through the Old Testament and New Testament. When His "fullness of time" (Gal. 4:4) had come to redeem a lost world through His Son, He gave 12 men to His Son to prepare them to accomplish His purposes.

When God is about to do something, He takes the initiative and comes to one or more of His servants. He lets them know what He is about to do. He invites them to adjust their lives to Him, so He can accomplish His work through them.

God takes the initiative to involve people in His work.

 Mark the following statements as T (true) or F (false).

____ 1. God created the world and then left it to function on its own.
____ 2. God is not absent. He is actively at work in the world.
____ 3. People do God's work by deciding on their own what they think would be good to do and then doing it.
____ 4. God involves people in His work.
____ 5. God always takes the initiative to involve people in His work.

I hope this is "review" material for you by now. Statements 2, 4, and 5 are true. The others are false.

God's Revelation Is Your Invitation

God's revelation is your invitation to join Him.

As God's *obedient* child, you are in a love relationship with Him. Because He loves you and wants to involve you in His work, He will show you where He is working so you can join Him. Jesus gave the example. He watched to see where the Father was at work. When He *saw*, He did what He saw the Father doing. When you see the Father at work around you, that is your invitation to adjust your life to Him and join Him in that work.

Elisha's servant

Is it possible for God to be working around you and you not see it? Yes. Elisha and his servant were in the city of Dothan surrounded by an army. The servant was terrified, but Elisha was calm. "Elisha prayed, 'O Lord, open his eyes so he may see.' Then the Lord opened the servant's eyes, and he looked and saw the hills full of horses and chariots of fire all around Elisha" (2 Kings 6:17). Only when the Lord opened the servant's eyes did he see God's activity.

Jerusalem's leaders

Jesus wept over Jerusalem and its leaders as He prophesied about the destruction that would take place in A.D. 70. He said, "If you, even you, had only known on this day what would bring you peace—but now it is hidden from your eyes" (Luke 19:42). God was in their midst preforming wonderful signs and miracles, but they did not recognize Him.

Two factors

Two factors are important for you to recognize the activity of God around you.
❏ You must be living in an intimate love relationship with God.
❏ God must take the initiative to open your spiritual eyes, so you can see what He is doing.

 Fill in the blank:

God's revelation to me of His activity is my _____ to join Him.

List two factors that are important for recognizing the activity of God around you.

1. _____

2. _____

When God reveals to you what He is doing around you, that is your invitation to join Him. Recognizing God's activity is dependent on your love relationship with Him and His taking the initiative to open your spiritual eyes to see it.

Working Where God Is at Work

Church planting

Our church sensed that God wanted us to help start new churches all across Canada. We had hundreds of towns that had no evangelical church.

 If you were in that situation, how would you go about deciding which towns to go to?

_____

Some churches would apply human logic to decide where the most promising and productive places might be. By now you know that we took a different approach. We tried to find out what God already was doing around us. We believed that He would show us where He was at work, and that revelation would be our invitation to join Him. We began praying and watching to see what God would do next in answer to our prayers.

Allan was a small town 40 miles from Saskatoon. It had never had a Protestant church. One of our members felt led to conduct a Vacation Bible School for the children in Allan. We said, "Let's find out if God is at work here."

So we conducted the Vacation Bible School. At the end of the week, we held a parents' night. We said to the group, "We believe God may want us to establish a Baptist church in this town. If any of you would like to begin a Bible study group and possibly be a part of a new church, would you just come forward."

From the back of the room came a lady. She was weeping. "I have prayed for 30 years that there would be a Baptist church in this town," she sobbed, "and you are the first people to respond."

Right behind her came an elderly man. "For years I was active in a Baptist church," he began. "Then I got into alcohol. Four years ago I came back to the Lord. I promised God that I would pray at least four hours every day until God brought us a Baptist church in our town. You are the first people to respond."

God had just shown us where He was at work! That was our invitation to join Him. We went back and joyfully shared with our church what God was doing. The church immediately voted to start a new church in Allan. As of today, that church in Allan has started one church and two mission churches.

If we will adjust our lives to God in a love relationship, He will show us where He is at work. That revelation is His invitation to us to get involved in His work. Then, when we join Him, He completes His work through us.

 Review today's lesson. Pray and ask God to identify one or more statements or Scriptures that He wants you to understand, learn, or practice. Underline it (them). Then respond to the following:

What was the most meaningful statement or Scripture you read today?

_____

Reword the statement or Scripture into a prayer of response to God.

_____

_____

What does God want you to do in response to today's study?

_____

"I have prayed for 30 years . . ."

"I promised God . . . I would pray four to five hours every day until God brought us a Baptist church in our town."

Work where God is at work.

SUMMARY STATEMENTS

• God is at work in the world.
• God takes the initiative to involve me in His work.
• God must take the initiative to open my spiritual eyes, so I can see what He is doing.
• When I see the Father at work around me, that is my invitation to adjust my life to Him and join Him in that work.
• God's revelation is my invitation to join Him.

KNOWING WHERE GOD IS AT WORK

There are some things only God can do.

If you are going to join God in His work, you need to know where God is working. The Scriptures tell us of some things only God can do. You need to learn to identify these. Then, when something happens around you that only God can do, you can know it is God's activity. This does not deny God's initiative. Unless God opens your spiritual eyes, you will not know He is at work.

Things Only God Can Do

The Scriptures say that no one can come to Christ except the Father draws him (John 6:44). No one will seek God or pursue spiritual things unless the Spirit of God is at work in his life. Suppose a neighbor, a friend, or a relative begins to ask about spiritual things. You do not have to question whether that is God drawing him or her. He is the only One who can do that. No one will ever seek after God unless God is at work in his life.

Zacchaeus

For example, as Jesus passed through a crowd, He was always looking for where the Father was at work. Jesus saw Zacchaeus in a tree. He may have said to Himself, "Nobody can seek after Me with that kind of earnestness unless My Father is at work in his heart." So Jesus pulled away from the crowd and said, "Zacchaeus, come down immediately. I must stay at your house today" (Luke 19:5). What happened? Salvation came to that household that night. Salvation came as a result of Jesus' joining His life to the activity of God.

 Read each of the Scriptures and answer the questions that follow.

> **John 14:15-17–**"If you love me, you will obey what I command. And I will ask the Father, and he will give you another Counselor to be with you forever—the Spirit of truth. . . . you know him, for he lives with you and will be in you."

1. If you love and obey Christ, whom will the Father give you? List two of His names.

_____

2. Where will this Person live?_____

> **John 14:26–**"The Counselor, the Holy Spirit, whom the Father will send in my name, will teach you all things and will remind you of everything I have said to you."

3. What are two things the Holy Spirit will do for Jesus' disciples?

_____

> **John 16:8–**"When he comes, he will convict the world of guilt in regard to sin and righteousness and judgment."

4. What are three more things the Holy Spirit does?

_____

_____

When you are saved, you enter a love relationship with Jesus Christ—God Himself. At that point the Holy Spirit comes to take up residence in your life. He is ever present to teach you.

Suppose you have a new friend at school who is not a Christian. You have a burden on your heart for this person. How would you find out what to do next?

_____

_____

You start by praying. Only the Father knows the best way to help your friend know about Christ. Pray, "Oh, God, show me where You are at work. Show me what You want me to do." After you pray, watch to see what God does next. Watch to see what this person is saying when he comes to you.

Pray and watch to see what God does next.

After you pray, you need to make the connection between your prayer and what happens next. If you do not connect what happens next, you may miss God's answer to your prayer. Always connect what happens next.

Make the connection.

Ask questions that will help reveal what is happening in the person's life. Learn to ask questions of people who cross your path to find out what God is doing in their lives. For instance:

Find out what God is already doing.

* How can I pray for you?
* What can I pray for you?
* Do you want to talk?
* What do you see as the greatest challenge in your life?
* What is the most significant thing happening in your life right now?
* Would you tell me what God is doing in your life?
* What particular burden has God given you?

Ask probing questions.

The person responds, "I really don't have a relationship with God. But lately, I sure have been thinking about it." Or "I used to go to Sunday School, but my whole family has quit going." Those statements sound like God is at work in that person's life. He may be drawing the person to Himself, causing the person to seek after God or bringing conviction of sin.

Listen.

 Answer the following questions:

A. What are some actions described in the previous paragraphs that will help you see if God is at work in a situation?

_____

_____

B. What would you watch for as you look for the activity of God in the lives of people around you? Complete this sentence to list three: I would watch for someone who . . .

1._____

2._____

3._____

What is God doing . . .

at your school?
where you work?
in your home?
in your church?

C. Write in the margin the names of people around you who are experiencing any of these activities of God in their lives.

Two More Points

We have spent two days focusing on the fact that God invites you to become involved in His work. You need to connect the following two points to this fact.

1. God speaks when He is about to accomplish His purposes. When God reveals to you what He is doing is when you need to respond. He speaks when He is about to accomplish His purposes. That is true throughout Scripture. Now,

1. God speaks when He is about to accomplish His purposes.

keep in mind the fact that the final completion may be a long time off. Abram's son was born 25 years after the promise from God. The time God comes to you, however, is the time for your response. You need to begin adjusting your life to Him. You may need to make some preparations for what He is about to do through you.

2. What God initiates, He completes.

2. What God initiates, He completes. Isaiah confirmed this when God said through him, "What I have said, that will I bring about; what I have planned, that will I do" (Isa. 46:11). Earlier he warned God's people, saying, "The Lord Almighty has sworn, 'Surely, as I have planned, so it will be, and as I have purposed, so it will stand. . . . For the Lord Almighty has purposed, and who can thwart him? His hand is stretched out, and who can turn it back?'" (Isa. 14:24, 27). God says that if He ever lets His people know what He is about to do, it is as good as done—He Himself will bring it to pass. (See also 1 Kings 8:56 and Phil. 1:6.)

God guarantees that, what He speaks, will happen. This holds enormous implications to individual believers, churches, and denominations. When we come to God to know what He is about to do where we are, we also come with the assurance that what God indicates He is about to do is certain to happen.

 Do you agree or disagree with the following statement? "What God initiates, He always completes." I Agree ❏ I Disagree ❏ Why? What is the reason for your response?

_____

You may have disagreed with the statement. Be sure you always base your understanding of God on Scripture, not on personal opinion or experience alone. Throughout history, people have said they have a word from the Lord and then it does not come to pass. You cannot look to these kinds of experiences to determine your understanding of God.

 Review today's lesson. Pray and ask God to identify one or more statements or Scriptures that He wants you to understand, learn, or practice. Underline it (them). Then respond to the following:

What was the most meaningful statement or Scripture you read today?

_____

Reword the statement or Scripture into a prayer of response to God.

_____

What does God want you to do in response to today's study?

_____

Be prepared to recite your memory verses to a partner in your group.

SUMMARY STATEMENTS

- A tender and sensitive heart will be ready to respond to God at the slightest prompting.
- Pray and watch to see what God does next.
- Make the connection. Ask probing questions. Listen.
- God speaks when He is about to accomplish His purposes.
- What God initiates, He completes.

GOD SPEAKS, PART 1

YOU'RE NOT NOAH

I asked Shannon how God spoke to her. She told her experience with such joy that I felt I needed to relay it to you in the same way she shared it with me. Here is what she said.

Okay, you want to hear a good one? I was in Sunday School class, and the guy leading the large-group session was talking about the importance of quiet times. He told us to take 1 Corinthians 13—the Love Chapter—and go off into a corner of the room, read it, and every time it says "Love," replace it with our name. "If the Lord convicts you about any one thing," he emphasized, "then close your eyes and pray about it."

The leader suggested that we begin with the last statement in chapter 12, Paul's introduction to the Love Chapter: "And now I will show you the most excellent way" (1 Cor. 12:29). Moving into chapter 13, I stayed a while at verse 4, substituting my name—"Shannon is patient; Shannon is kind." Yeah, okay, I'm that most of the time. No conviction yet (big sigh). Shannon is not jealous; Shannon does not brag and is not arrogant. Right there is where I got convicted.

I didn't realize, for sure, that I was boastful; but I closed my eyes anyway and prayed about it. I got this picture in my head of Noah's Ark, like an illustration out of a children's Bible. I thought *Noah's Ark? That's weird, God.* And then I got it. It was like God was saying, "You're not Noah."

You see, everything had been going great in my life. Me and my sister had been singing at other churches and practicing a lot. My quiet times had been great. In fact, everything this guy was saying in class, I was already doing. But, at that moment, I realized I had been feeling just a little more superior and more spiritual than everyone else.

It was so clear to me that God was telling me I wasn't Noah. I wasn't the only one God was speaking to. That was weird, because it was about the clearest God had ever spoken to me. He really got through to me.

Thank you, Shannon, for letting God speak through you to me.

He who belongs to God hears what God says.
The reason you do not hear is that you do not
belong to God.

—JOHN 8:47

*Verse to Memorize
This Week*

GOD SPEAKS IN DIFFERENT WAYS

If the Christian does not know when God is speaking, he is in trouble at the heart of his Christian life!

One critical point to understanding and experiencing God is *knowing clearly when God is speaking*. If the Christian does not know when God is speaking, he is in trouble at the *heart* of his Christian life! In this unit we will focus our attention on how God speaks through the Holy Spirit to reveal Himself, His purposes, and His ways. We will examine ways God speaks through the Bible, prayer, circumstances, and the church or other believers.

Many Different Ways

In the Old Testament God spoke in many different ways.

The fact that God spoke is the most important factor.

"In the past God spoke to our forefathers through the prophets at many times and in various ways" (Heb. 1:1). One truth that is evident throughout the Bible is that God speaks to His people. In the Old Testament, God spoke through angels, a gentle whisper, visions, dreams, miraculous signs, and other ways. But *how* God spoke in the Old Testament is not the most important factor. The fact that He spoke is the crucial point. Those He spoke to *knew* it was God, and they *knew* what He was saying.

 Which is most important?   How God spoke ❑   That God spoke ❑

When God spoke to a person in the Old Testament what two things did the person know? He or she knew . . .

_____

Four Important Factors

I see four important factors each time God spoke in the Old Testament. The burning bush experience of Moses in Exodus 3 is an example.

Unique to the individual

1. **When God spoke, it was usually unique to that individual.** For instance, Moses had no reason to expect a burning bush experience. God had not spoken to anyone that way before. God spoke that way because He wanted the experience to be personal to Moses. That has not changed.

 What is the first important factor in the way God spoke to individuals in the Old Testament?

1. _____

Sure God was speaking

2. **When God spoke, the person was sure God was speaking.** The Scriptures testify that Moses was sure his encounter was with God (Ex. 5:1). Could Moses logically prove to someone that he had heard from God? No. All he could do was testify to his encounter with God. Only God could cause His people to know that the word He gave Moses was a word from the God of their fathers.

 What is the second important factor in the way God spoke in the Old Testament?

2. _____

Knew what God said

3. **When God spoke, the person knew what God said.** Moses knew what God was telling him to do. He knew how God wanted to work through him.

 What is the third important factor in the way God spoke in the Old Testament?

3. _____

4. *When God spoke, that was the encounter with God.* Moses would have been foolish to say, "This has been a wonderful experience at this burning bush. I hope this leads me to an encounter with God!" That *was* the encounter with God! When God reveals truth to you, by whatever means, that is an encounter with God. God is the only One who can cause you to experience His presence.

 What is the fourth important factor in the way God spoke in the Old Testament?

4. _____

Using the "hints" below, see if you can write the four factors you just read about.

1. Unique _____

2. Sure _____

3. What _____

4. Encounter _____

A Wrong Pattern

I hear many people say something like this: "Lord, I really want to know your will. Stop me if I am wrong and bless me if I am right." The only problem is I don't see this as a pattern anywhere in the Scriptures.

You cannot allow yourself to be guided by experience alone. You also cannot allow yourself to be guided by tradition, a method, or a formula. Often people trust in these ways because they are easy. They do as they please and put the whole burden of responsibility on God. If they are wrong, He must intervene and stop them. If they make a mistake, they blame Him.

If you want to know the will and voice of God, you must give the time and effort to cultivate a love relationship with Him. That is what He wants!

Which of the following is the scriptural pattern for knowing God's will? Check one.

❏ Look for open and closed doors.
❏ Ask God to stop you if you are wrong.
❏ Wait until you hear a clear word from God.

The pattern I see in Scripture is that God always gives a direction on the front end. He may not tell you all you want to know at the beginning, but He will tell you what you need to know to take the first step of obedience. Your task is to wait until the Master gives you instructions. If you start "doing" before you have a direction from God, more than likely you will be wrong.

Specific Directions

A popular teaching says God does not give you clear directions. It says He just sets your life in motion; then you try to figure out the directions. This implies that a Christian always thinks correctly and according to God's will. The teaching does not take into account the fact that the old nature is constantly battling with the spiritual nature (Rom. 7). Only God can give you the kind of specific directions to accomplish His purposes *in His ways.*

After God spoke to Noah about building an ark, Noah knew the size, the type of materials, and how to put it together. When God spoke to Moses about building the tabernacle He was very specific about the details. When God became flesh in the Person of Jesus Christ, He gave specific directions to His disciples—where to go, what to do, how to respond.

What about when God told Abraham (Abram) to "go to the land I will show you" (Gen. 12:1)? That was not very specific. But God did say, "I will show you." God will give you enough specific directions to do *now* what He wants you to do. When you need more directions, He gives you more according to His timing.

Just as God gave clear directions in Old Testament times, the Holy Spirit gives clear directions today. You may say, "That has not been my experience." You need to: Base your understanding of God on Scripture, not on experience.

Base your understanding of God on Scripture, not on experience.

 Underline the suggestions in the following paragraph that will help you as you look to God for direction in your life.

If you do not have clear instructions from God in a matter, pray and wait. Depend on God's timing. His timing is always right and best. Don't get in a hurry. He may be withholding directions to cause you to seek Him more intently. Don't try to skip over the relationship to get on with *doing*. God is more interested in a love relationship with you than He is in what you can do for Him.

In your own words summarize the directions you underlined.

_____

Review today's lesson. Pray and ask God to identify one or more statements or Scriptures that He wants you to understand, learn, or practice. Underline it (them). Then respond to the following:

What was the most meaningful statement or Scripture you read today?

_____

Reword the statement or Scripture into a prayer of response to God.

_____

What does God want you to do in response to today's study?

_____

Write your Scripture memory verse for this unit on the following lines and review verses from other units.

_____

_____

SUMMARY STATEMENTS

- If I do not know when God is speaking, I am in trouble at the heart of my Christian life!
- *That* God spoke to people is far more important than *how* He spoke.
- When God spoke, it was usually unique to that individual.
- When God spoke, the person was sure it was God.
- When God spoke, the person knew what God said.
- When God spoke, that was the encounter with God.
- If I do not have clear instructions from God in a matter, I will pray and wait. I will not try to bypass the love relationship.

GOD SPEAKS BY THE HOLY SPIRIT

Hebrews 1:1-2 says, "In the past God spoke to our forefathers through the prophets at many times and in various ways, but in these last days he has spoken to us by his Son."

In the Gospels . . .

In the Gospels God spoke through His Son—Jesus. The Gospel of John begins: "In the beginning was the Word, and the Word was with God, and the Word was God . . . . The Word became flesh and made his dwelling among us" (John 1:1, 14). God became flesh in the Person of Jesus Christ. (See also 1 John 1:1-4.)

God spoke by His Son.

The disciples didn't understand. Philip even said, "Lord, show us the Father and that will be enough for us" (John 14:8).

Jesus responded, "Don't you know me, Philip, even after I have been among you such a long time? Anyone who has seen me has seen the Father. . . . The words I say to you are not just my own. Rather, it is the Father, living in me, who is doing his work" (John 14:9-10). When Jesus spoke, the Father was speaking through Him. When Jesus did a miracle, the Father was doing His work through Jesus.

Just as Moses was face-to-face with God at the burning bush, the disciples were face-to-face with God in a personal relationship with Jesus. Their encounter with Jesus *was* an encounter with God. To hear from Jesus *was* to hear from God.

 Write a summary statement of how God spoke during the life of Jesus.

_____

When the disciples heard Jesus, they heard God. When Jesus spoke, that was an encounter with God.

In Acts and to the Present . . .

When we move from the Gospels to Acts and to the present, we often change our whole way of thinking. We live as if God quit speaking personally to His people. We fail to realize that an encounter with the Holy Spirit *is* an encounter with God. God clearly spoke to His people in Acts. He clearly speaks to us today. From Acts to the present, God has been speaking to His people by the Holy Spirit.

God speaks by the Holy Spirit.

The Holy Spirit takes up residence in the life of a believer. "You yourselves are God's temple and . . . God's Spirit lives in you" (1 Cor. 3:16). "Your body is a temple of the Holy Spirit, who is in you, whom you have received from God" (1 Cor. 6:19). Because He is always present in a believer, He can speak to you clearly and at anytime.

We have already studied about God's speaking to His people. Here are some of the key ideas we examined:
- In the Old Testament God spoke in many different ways.
- In the Gospels God spoke through His Son.
- In Acts and to the present God speaks by the Holy Spirit.
- God speaks by the Holy Spirit through the Bible, prayer, circumstances, and the church to reveal Himself, His purposes, and His ways.
- Knowing God's voice comes from an intimate love relationship with God.
- God speaks when He has a purpose in mind for your life.
- The moment God speaks to you is the moment He wants you to respond to Him.
- The moment God speaks to you is God's timing.

Review "God Speaks"

Answer the following questions.

1. How did God speak in the Old Testament?

_____

2. How did God speak in the Gospels?

_____

3. How did God speak in Acts and to the present time?

_____

4. How do you come to know God's voice?

_____

5. How do you know God's timing?

_____

Check your answers in the preceding review list.

Encountering God

An encounter with the Holy Spirit is an encounter with God.

When God spoke to Moses and others in the Old Testament, those events *were* encounters with God. An encounter with Jesus *was* an encounter with God for the disciples. In the same way, an encounter with the Holy Spirit is an encounter with God for you.

You never discover truth. Truth is revealed.

Now that the Holy Spirit is given, He is the One who guides you into all truth and teaches you all things. You understand spiritual truth because the Holy Spirit is working in your life. You cannot understand the Word of God unless the Spirit of God teaches you. When you come to the Word of God, the Author Himself is present to instruct you. You never *discover* truth; truth is *revealed*. When the Holy Spirit reveals truth to you, He is not leading you to an encounter with God. That is an encounter with God!

 Has God been speaking to you during this course? Yes ❏ No ❏ As a review, look back through the lesson-review activities in Units 1-4.
- **Read through the statements or Scriptures that God called to your attention.**
- **Read and pray again the prayer responses.**
- **Review the things you sensed God wanted you to do in response to the lessons.**

Briefly summarize what you sense God has been saying to you this far in the course. Focus on the general themes or directions rather than specific details.

_____

_____

Have you been responding to what God has been calling to your attention? How would you describe your response to His leading?

_____

_____

What do you sense is your greatest spiritual challenge right now?

_____

Without looking, try to quote the first four statements of the realities of experiencing God. Use these hints: work, relationship, invitation, speaks. Check yourself using the inside back cover or quote them to another person and ask him to check your answers.

Immediately Respond

When God spoke to Moses, what Moses did next was crucial. After Jesus spoke to the disciples, what they did next was crucial. What you do next after the Spirit of God speaks to you through His Word is crucial. Our problem is that when the Spirit of God speaks to us, we go into a long discussion. Moses went into a long discussion with God (Ex. 3:11—4:13), and it limited him for the rest of his life. Moses had to speak to the people through his brother Aaron (Ex. 4:14-16).

I challenge you to review what you sense God has been saying to you on a regular basis. If God speaks and you hear but do not respond, a time could come when you will not hear His voice. Disobedience can lead to a "famine of hearing the words of the Lord" (Amos 8:11-12).

When Samuel was a young boy, God began to speak to him. The Scriptures say, "The Lord was with Samuel as he grew up, and he let none of his words fall to the ground" (1 Sam. 3:19). Be like Samuel. Don't let a single word from the Lord fail to bring adjustments in your life. Then God will do in you and through you everything He says to you.

"The Lord was with Samuel as he grew up, and he let none of his words fall to the ground."
—1 Samuel 3:19

In Luke 8:5-15, Jesus told the parable of the sower and the seeds. The seed that fell on the good soil represented one who heard the word of God, kept it in his heart, and produced fruit. Then Jesus said, "Consider carefully how you listen. Whoever has will be given more; whoever does not have, even what he thinks he has will be taken from him" (Luke 8:18). If you hear the word of God and do not apply it to produce fruit in your life, even what you think you have will be taken away. Be careful how you listen to God! Make up your mind now that when the Spirit of God speaks to you, you are going to do what He says.

Review today's lesson. Pray and ask God to identify one or more statements or Scriptures that He wants you to understand, learn, or practice. Underline it (them). Then respond to the following:

What was the most meaningful statement or Scripture you read today?

_____

Reword the statement or Scripture into a prayer of response to God.

_____

What does God want you to do in response to today's study?

_____

SUMMARY STATEMENTS
- An encounter with the Holy Spirit is an encounter with God.
- I understand spiritual truth because the Holy Spirit is working in my life.
- When I come to the Word of God, the Author Himself is present to instruct me.
- I never *discover* truth; truth is *revealed*.

DAY 3

GOD REVEALS

God's revelations are designed to bring you into a love relationship with Him.

God speaks to His people. When He speaks, what does He reveal? Throughout the Scriptures, when God speaks, it is to reveal something about Himself, His purposes, or His ways. God's revelations are designed to bring you into a love relationship with Him.

God Reveals Himself

When God speaks to you by the Holy Spirit, He often reveals something about Himself. He reveals His name. He reveals His nature and character.

 Read these Scriptures. After each one, write what God revealed about Himself.

"When Abram was ninety-nine years old, the Lord . . . said, 'I am God Almighty'" (Gen. 17:1). _____

"The Lord said to Moses, 'Speak to the entire assembly of Israel and say to them: "Be holy because I, the Lord your God, am holy" ' " (Lev. 19:1-2). _____

"'I the Lord do not change . . . . Ever since the time of your forefathers you have turned away from my decrees and have not kept them. Return to me, and I will return to you,' says the Lord Almighty." (Mal. 3:6-7). _____

"Jesus said to the Jews, 'I am the living bread that came down from heaven. If anyone eats of this bread, he will live forever'" (John 6:51). _____

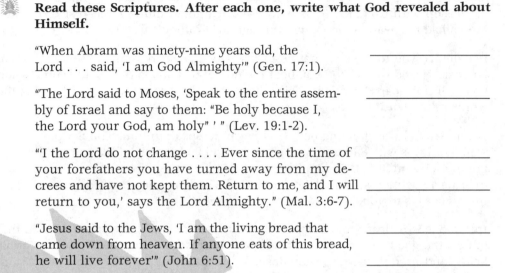

God revealed Himself to Abram by His name—God Almighty. To Moses He revealed His holy nature. God spoke through Malachi to Israel and revealed that He is unchanging and forgiving. Jesus revealed Himself as "living bread" and the source of eternal life.

God reveals Himself to increase my faith.

God speaks when He wants to involve someone in His work. He reveals Himself in order to help the person respond in faith. The person can better respond to God's instructions when he believes God is who He says He is, and when he believes God can do what He says He will do.

Stop for a minute and meditate on why God revealed Himself as He did to each person mentioned in the Scriptures above. When you think you have an idea of why each revelation was given, read on.

• Ninety-nine-year-old Abram needed to know God was almighty (all powerful, able to do anything), so He could believe that God could give him a son in his old age.
• Through Moses, God said He was holy. His people had to believe He was holy, so they would respond by being holy themselves.
• Through Malachi, God revealed His forgiving nature, so the people could believe that they would be forgiven if they would return to God.
• Jesus revealed that He was the source of eternal life, so the Jews could believe and respond to Him and receive life.

Why does God reveal Himself (His name, His nature, His character)?

_____

_____

God reveals Himself to increase faith that leads to action. You will need to listen attentively to what God reveals to you about Himself. This will be critical when you come to the crisis of belief.

• You will have to believe God is who He says He is.
• You will have to believe God can do what He says He will do.
• You will have to adjust your thinking in light of this belief.

 When God speaks by the Holy Spirit, what is one thing He reveals?

God speaks by the Holy Spirit to reveal _____, His purposes, and His ways.

God Reveals His Purposes

God reveals His purposes so you will know what He plans to do. If you are to join Him, you need to know what God is about to do. This point should be a review for you (see pp. 36-38).

God reveals His purposes so I will do His work.

When God came to Noah He did not ask, "What do you want to do for me?" He came to reveal what He was about to do. It was far more important to know what *God* was about to do. It really did not matter what Noah had planned to do for God. God was about to destroy the world. He wanted to work through Noah to accomplish *His* purposes of saving a remnant of people and animals to repopulate the earth.

Noah

Similarly, God came to Abram and spoke to him because He had a purpose in mind. He was preparing to build a nation for Himself. God was about to accomplish His purposes through Abram.

Abram

This sequence is seen throughout the Bible (the Judges, David, the prophets, the disciples, and Paul): When God was about to do something, *He* took the initiative to come to His servants (Amos 3:7). He spoke to reveal His purposes and plans. Then He could involve them and accomplish *His* purposes through them.

"Surely the Sovereign Lord does nothing without revealing his plan to his servants the prophets."
—Amos 3:7

In contrast, we set about to dream our dreams of what WE want to do for God. Then we make long-range plans based on priorities of *our* choosing. What is important is what *God* plans to do where we are and how He wants to accomplish it through us. Look what the Psalmist said about our plans and purposes:

> The Lord foils the plans of the nations;
>   he thwarts the purposes of the peoples.
> But the plans of the Lord stand firm forever,
>   the purposes of his heart through all generations.
>   —Psalm 33:10-11

 Read Proverbs 19:21 (right) and Psalm 33:10-11 (above). Why does God reveal His purposes?

"Many are the plans in a man's heart, but it is the Lord's purpose that prevails."
—Proverbs 19:21

_____

Based on Psalm 33:10-11, answer the following questions.

1. What does the Lord do to the plans of the nations?

_____

2. What does the Lord do to the purposes of the peoples?

_____

3. What happens to the plans and purposes of the Lord?

_____

God's purposes
versus
our plans

For Review see
pages 27-29.

Do you see why you need to know God's plans and purposes? Your plans and purposes must be God's plans and purposes, or you will not experience God working through you. God reveals His purposes so you will know what He plans to do. Then you can join Him.

God wants us to follow *Him* daily, not just follow a plan. If we try to spell out all the details of His will in a planning session, we have a tendency to think: "Now that we know where we are going and how to get there, *we* can get the job done." Then we forget about the need for the daily relationship with God. We may set about to accomplish our plans and forget the relationship. God created us for an eternal love relationship. Life is our opportunity to experience Him at work.

Planning is not all wrong. Just be very careful not to plan more than God intends for you to plan. Let God interrupt or redirect your plans any time He wants. Remain in a close relationship with Him so you can always hear His voice when He wants to speak to you.

 When God speaks by the Holy Spirit, what are two things He reveals?

God speaks by the Holy Spirit to reveal _____, His _____, and His ways.

God Reveals His Ways

God reveals His ways so I can accomplish His purposes.

Even the casual or uninformed reader of the Bible can see that God's ways and plans are so different from those of people. God uses *Kingdom* principles to accomplish Kingdom purposes. God reveals His ways to us because they are the only way to accomplish His purposes.

"My thoughts are not your thoughts, neither are your ways my ways."
—Isaiah 55:8

God said, "My thoughts are not your thoughts, neither are your ways my ways" (Isa. 55:8). God does not work in human ways. We will not accomplish God's work in our own ways. This is one of the basic sin problems people face: "We all, like sheep, have gone astray, each of us has turned to his own way" (Isa. 53:6).

 Why does God reveal His ways?

_____

Our ways may seem good to us. We may achieve some moderate successes. When we try to do the work of God in our own ways, however, we will never see the mighty power of God in what we do. God reveals His ways because that is the only way to accomplish His purposes. When God accomplishes His purposes in His ways through us, people will come to know God. They will recognize that, what has happened, can only be explained by God.

Using Kingdom ways, Jesus fed 5,000. (Matt. 14:13-21)

Jesus demonstrated Kingdom ways for the disciples. He asked them to feed the multitudes. The disciples' response was, "Send them home!" Jesus, using *Kingdom* principles, told the crowd to sit down, then fed them and had baskets full of leftovers. They saw the Father work a miracle. What a contrast! The disciples would have sent the people home empty and hungry. God displayed to a watching world His love, His nature, and His power. This kind of display would draw people to Himself through His Son Jesus. This kind of mighty display happened many times in the lives of the disciples. They had to learn to function according to *Kingdom* principles to do *Kingdom* work.

God gets the glory

God's purposes accomplished in His ways bring glory to Him. You must learn to do Kingdom work in Kingdom ways. "Come, let us go up to the mountain of the Lord . . . . He will teach us his ways, so that we may walk in his paths" (Mic. 4:2).

When God speaks by the Holy Spirit, what are three things He reveals?

God speaks by the Holy Spirit to reveal _____,
His _____ and His _____.

Match the things God reveals with the reason.

God reveals . . .	Because . . .
____ 1. Himself	A. He wants me to know how to accomplish things only He can do.
____ 2. His purposes	B. He wants me to know what He is about to do so I can join Him.
____ 3. His ways	C. He wants me to have faith to believe He can do what He says.

Answers to the matching activity are: 1-C, 2-B, 3-A.

When I was first learning how to walk with God, I depended too much on other people. I would run to other people and say, "Do you think this is really God? Here is what I think. What do you think?" I would unconsciously, or consciously, depend on them rather than on the relationship I had with God.

Finally I had to say, "I am going to go to the Lord and clarify what I am absolutely convinced He is saying to me. Then, I am going to proceed and watch to see how God affirms it." I began that process over a period of time in many areas of my life. My love relationship with God became all important. I began to discover a clear, personal way in which God was making known His ways to me. God revealed His ways to me through His Word. Tomorrow we will look at how God speaks through His Word. In future lessons we will look at how God speaks through prayer, circumstances, and the church to confirm His will to us.

Review today's lesson. Pray and ask God to identify one or more statements or Scriptures that He wants you to understand, learn, or practice. Underline it (them). Then respond to the following:

What was the most meaningful statement or Scripture you read today?

_____

Reword the statement or Scripture into a prayer of response to God.

_____

What does God want you to do in response to today's study?

_____

Practice quoting your Scripture memory verses aloud.

SUMMARY STATEMENTS

- God's revelations are designed to bring me into a love relationship with Him.
- God reveals Himself to increase my faith.
- God reveals His purposes so I will do His work.
- God reveals His ways so I can accomplish His purposes.

GOD SPEAKS THROUGH THE BIBLE

"His sheep . . . know his voice."
—*John 10:4*

God speaks to you by the Holy Spirit to reveal Himself, His purposes, and His ways. Perhaps the questions people ask most about God's speaking are:
- How does God speak to me?
- How can I know when God is speaking?
- How can God be more real and personal to me?

God speaks uniquely to individuals, and He can do it in any way He pleases. As you walk in an intimate love relationship with God, you will come to recognize His voice. You will know when God is speaking to you.

Jesus compared the relationship He has with His followers to the relationship a shepherd has with his sheep. He said, "The man who enters by the gate is the shepherd of his sheep . . . . the sheep listen to his voice . . . . his sheep follow him because they know his voice" (John 10:2-4). In just this way, when God speaks to you, you will recognize His voice and follow Him.

God speaks in many ways. In the present, God primarily speaks by the Holy Spirit through the Bible, prayer, circumstances, and the church. These four means are difficult to separate. God uses prayer and the Bible together. Often circumstances and the church, or other believers, will help confirm what God is saying to you. Frequently, God uses circumstances and the church to help you know His timing. We will talk more about that in the next unit. Today, I want us to look at how God speaks through the Bible.

Mark the following statements as T (true) or F (false).

_____ 1. God can uniquely speak to individuals any way He chooses.

_____ 2. In the present, God primarily speaks through dreams and visions.

_____ 3. When rightly related to God, His people will hear and recognize His voice.

_____ 4. God often speaks by the Holy Spirit through the Bible and prayer.

God is sovereign. He can do whatever He chooses to do. With the Scripture as our guide, we know God can speak in unique ways to individuals. His people will hear and recognize His voice. In the present time, He primarily speaks by the Holy Spirit through the Bible, prayer, circumstances, and the church. Only item 2 is false. The others are true.

The Spirit of Truth

The Bible is God's Word. It describes God's complete revelation of Himself to humanity. God speaks to you through the Bible. As you have already learned, however, a person cannot understand spiritual truth unless the Spirit of God reveals it. The Holy Spirit is "the Spirit of truth" (John 14:17). The diagram on the next page should help you visualize how the Holy Spirit speaks to you through God's Word. Look at the diagram as you read the following explanation.

When the Holy Spirit reveals a spiritual truth from the Word of God, He is personally relating to your life. That is an encounter with God. The sequence is this:
1. You read the Word of God—the Bible.
2. The Spirit of Truth takes the Word of God and reveals truth.
3. You adjust your life to the truth of God.
4. You obey Him.
5. God works in and through you to accomplish His purposes.

 Using the description on page 80 and the diagram above, write a summary of how God speaks through the Bible.

_____

_____

Write the following key words in the correct sequence: *adjust, reveals, obey, read.*

1. I _____ the Word of God—the Bible.

2. The Spirit of Truth takes the Word of God and _____ a truth.

3. I _____ my life to the truth of God.

4. I _____ Him.

5. God works in and through me to accomplish His purposes.

Check your work.

The Spirit uses the Word of God (the sword of the Spirit—Eph. 6:17) to reveal God and His purposes. The Spirit uses the Word of God to instruct us in the ways of God. On our own we cannot understand the truths of God. Unaided by the Spirit of God, it will be foolishness to us (1 Cor. 2:14). Aided by the Spirit, we can understand all things (1 Cor. 2:15).

 Respond to the following:

God probably has used a particular verse of Scripture to speak to you at some time during this course. Look back through Units 1-5 and find one passage of Scripture that God seems to have called to your attention. What is the verse?

_____

1. What does that verse reveal to you about God, His purposes, or His ways?

_____

_____

_____

"The man without the Spirit does not accept the things that come from the Spirit of God, for they are foolishness to him, and he cannot understand them, because they are spiritually discerned. The spiritual man makes judgments about all things."

—1 Corinthians 2:14-15

2. Meditate on this verse and pray. Ask God to continue speaking to you about the truth in this passage. Keep in mind that He is more interested in what you become than what you do.

3. What does God want to do or be in and through your life?

_____

4. What adjustments would you have to make to align your life with this truth in:

   Your personal life? _____

   Your family life? _____

   Your church life? _____

   Your school life? _____

5. Write a prayer response to God concerning this truth and its application to your life.

_____

6. Since you first came to understand this truth, has God done anything in your life that required you to apply the truth or share it with someone else? Yes ❑ No ❑ If so, what?

_____

Understanding spiritual truth does not lead you to an encounter with God; it is the encounter with God.

Understanding spiritual truth does not lead you *to* an encounter with God; it *is* the encounter with God. You cannot understand the purposes and ways of God, unless the Spirit of God teaches you. If God has revealed spiritual truth to you through this passage of Scripture, you have encountered God Himself working in you!

Responding to Truth

Reading Scripture is an exciting time of anticipation for me. The Spirit of God knows the mind of God. He knows what God is ready to do in my life. The Spirit of God then begins to open my understanding about God and His purposes and His ways. I take that very seriously.

When God leads you to a fresh understanding of Himself or His ways through Scripture:
• Write down the verse(s) in a spiritual journal or diary.
• Meditate on the verse.
• Study it to immerse yourself in the meaning of the verse. What is God revealing about Himself, His purpose, or His ways?
• Identify the adjustments you need to make in your personal, family, church, and school life, so God can work that way with you.
• Write a prayer response to God.
• Make the necessary adjustments to God.
• Watch to see how God may use that truth about Himself in your life during the day.

Here is an illustration of the way God may use His Word to speak to you. Suppose you are reading your daily Bible reading from Psalm 37. You have read this Psalm many times before. You come to verse 21 and read: "The wicked borrow and do not repay." You are "drawn" back to that verse. You read it again. Then you remember a debt you have failed to repay. You realize that this Scripture applies to you.

The Holy Spirit has just spoken to you through that verse. You have encountered truth. Now you understand that those who borrow and do not repay are wicked in God's sight. The Holy Spirit has called your attention to a specific instance where this verse applies to you. He is convicting you of sin. He is the only One who can do that. God has just spoken to you by the working of the Holy Spirit and through His Word. God wants you to have no hindrances to a love relationship with Him in your life.

 If you were in this situation, what should you do next? Following the sequence in the diagram on page 81, what do you do after the Holy Spirit reveals an understanding of truth to you?

_____

Once God has spoken to you through His Word, how you respond is crucial. You must adjust your life to the truth. In this case the adjustment is this:

Adjust

• You must *agree* with the truth—those who borrow and do not repay are wicked in God's sight.
• You must *agree* that the truth applies to you in the particular instance brought to your memory. This is confession of sin. You *agree* with God about your sin.

In this way you have adjusted your understanding about borrowing and repaying to agree with God's will in this matter. To agree with God you must change your understanding to agree with His. This requires an adjustment. Is that all you must do? No! Agreeing with God is not enough. Until you repay the debt, you will continue to be seen as wicked in God's sight. This is where obedience comes in. You obey God's will by repaying the debt.

Obey

Now you are free to experience a more complete relationship with God. Always tie a revealed truth to your understanding of God and your relationship with Him.

 Review today's lesson. Pray and ask God to identify one or more statements or Scriptures that He wants you to understand, learn, or practice. Underline it (them). Then respond to the following:

What was the most meaningful statement or Scripture you read today?

_____

Reword the statement or Scripture into a prayer of response to God.

_____

What does God want you to do in response to today's study?

_____

SUMMARY STATEMENTS

• God speaks uniquely to individuals, and He can do it in any way He pleases.
• When God speaks to me, I will recognize His voice and follow Him.
• I cannot understand spiritual truth unless the Spirit of God reveals it.

DAY 5

GOD SPEAKS THROUGH PRAYER

If you are not keeping a spiritual journal[1], or diary, you need to. When God speaks to you in your quiet time, immediately write down what He said before you have time to forget. Then record your prayer response.

Truth Is a Person

 Carefully read the following paragraphs and fill in the blanks in the key statements that follow.

"I am the truth."
—*Jesus*

The Holy Spirit reveals truth. Truth is not just some concept to be studied. Truth is a Person. Jesus did not say, "I will teach you the truth." He said, "I am . . . the truth" (John 14:6).

When God gives you eternal life, He gives you Himself (John 17:3). When the Holy Spirit reveals Truth, He is not teaching you a concept to be thought about. He is leading you to a relationship with a Person. *He* is your life! When you became a Christian, Jesus didn't give you some *thing*; He gave you Himself.

Fill in the blanks with the correct words from the previous paragraphs

1. The Holy Spirit reveals _____.

2. Truth is not just some _____ to be studied.

3. Truth is a _____.

4. The Holy Spirit is leading you to a _____ with a Person.

My relationship to God

Here is a summary of how I have tried to live out my relationship with God:
• God creates in me the desire to participate in His mission to reconcile a lost world to Himself.
• I respond and come to God seeking to know His will.
• When God reveals a truth to me, I know He is trying to alert me to what He is doing in my life.

The Author is telling me what He is doing in my life.

When God reveals truth to me through His Word, that doesn't lead me to an encounter with God; that *is* the encounter with God. When He does reveal truth to me, I sit in the presence of a living Person, the Author of the Scriptures. The Author is telling me what He is doing in my life, and He uses His Word to do it.

The Spirit of God knows the mind of God. He will make the will of God known to me through the Word of God. I must then take that truth and immediately adjust my life to Him. I do not adjust my life to a concept or a philosophy but to a Person.

Have you ever read a Scripture you have read many times before, but suddenly you see something in it for the first time? That truth is not a concept for you to figure out how to work into your life. God is introducing you to Himself and alerting you to the reality that He wants to apply this truth to your life right now.

Prayer Is a Relationship

Your personal prayer life may primarily be one-way communication—you talking to God. Prayer is more than that, though. Prayer includes listening as well. It is two-way fellowship and communication with God. You speak to God, and He speaks to you.

Prayer is a relationship, not just a religious activity. Prayer is designed to adjust you to God, rather than to adjust God to you. God doesn't need your prayers, but He wants you to pray. You need to pray because of what God wants to do in and through your life during your praying. God speaks to His people by the Holy Spirit through prayer. Here is a diagram of how God speaks through prayer.

Prayer is a relationship, not just a religious activity.

This diagram illustrates an encounter with God. When the Holy Spirit reveals a spiritual truth to you in prayer, He is present and working actively in your life. What happens as you seek God's will in prayer? The sequence is this:

1. God takes the initiative by causing you to want to pray.
2. The Holy Spirit takes the Word of God and reveals to you the will of God.
3. In the Spirit you pray in agreement with the will of God.
4. You adjust your life to the truth (to God).
5. You look and listen for confirmation or further direction from the Bible, circumstances, and the church (other believers).
6. You obey.
7. God works in you and through you to accomplish His purposes.

 Read back through the previous list and circle a key word or phrase in each statement.

The Spirit of God uses the Word of God when you pray. I find that, when I pray about something, Scripture often comes to my mind. I believe the Spirit of God is trying to guide me through the Scripture. I have found that, as I pray about a particular matter, He takes the Word of God and applies it to my heart and my mind to reveal the truth. I immediately stop my praying and open the Word of God to the passage I believe the Spirit of God brought to my mind.

Praying in the Spirit

The Spirit of God will take the Word of God to guide you in your praying.

 Read the passage in the margin and answer the following questions.
   1. Why do we need the help of the Holy Spirit when we pray? (v. 26)

_____

_____

"The Spirit helps us in our weakness. We do not know what we ought to pray for, but the Spirit himself intercedes for us with groans that words cannot express. And he who searches our hearts knows the mind of the Spirit, because the Spirit intercedes for the saints in accordance with God's will."
—Romans 8:26-27

2. What advantage does the Holy Spirit have that we do not have? (v. 27)

_____

3. What does the Holy Spirit do for us?

_____

We are weak and do not know how we ought to pray. The Holy Spirit has an advantage over us—He already knows the will of God. When He prays for us, He is praying absolutely in agreement with the will of God. He then helps us know the will of God as we pray.

What happens when you pray? The Holy Spirit knows what God has in mind for you. His task is to get you to want it—to get you to ask for it. What will happen when you ask for things God already wants to give or do? You will always receive them. Why? Because you have asked *according to the will of God*. When God answers your prayer, He gets the glory, and your faith is increased.

"It is God who works in you to will and to act according to his good purpose."
—Philippians 2:13

How do you know what the Holy Spirit is saying? I cannot give you a formula. I can tell you that you will know His voice when He speaks (John 10:4). You must decide, however, that you only want His will. You must dismiss any selfish or fleshly desires of your own. Then, as you start to pray, the Spirit of God starts to touch your heart and cause you to pray in the direction of God's will (Phil. 2:13).

Write down what God is saying.

I always write down what God is saying to me when I pray and as I read His Word. I write down what I sense He is leading me to pray. As I begin to see what God is telling me about Himself, His purposes, and His ways, I often see a pattern begin to develop. As I watch the direction the Spirit is leading me to pray, I begin to get a clear indication of what God is saying to me. This process calls for spiritual concentration!

You may be asking the question: But how do I know that the directions I am praying are the Spirit's leading and not my own selfish desires? Do you remember what George Mueller said he does first in seeking God's directions?

 Look back at item 1 on page 31. What did he do in the beginning?

_____

Deny self

Deny self first. In all honesty with yourself and before God, come to the place where you are sure that your only desire is to know God's will alone. Then check to see what the Holy Spirit is saying in other ways. Ask yourself:
• What is He saying to me in His Word?
• What is He saying to me in prayer?
• How is He confirming it through circumstances?
• How is He confirming it through the counsel of other believers?

God never will lead you in opposition to His written Word. If what you sense in prayer runs contrary to Scriptures, it is wrong. For instance, God will never, never lead you to steal or take drugs. He always is opposed to that kind of behavior. Watch for God to use the written Word to confirm what you are sensing in prayer. Don't play games with God, though. Don't just look for a Scripture that seems to say what *you* selfishly want to do, and then claim it is God's will. That is very dangerous. Don't do it.

 Look back at the diagram and try to summarize what it illustrates. Write a summary of how God speaks through prayer.

_____

Write the following key words in the correct sequence: *adjust, confirmation, Word, initiative, agreement, obey.* If you need help look at the list following the prayer diagram (p. 85).

1. God takes the _____ by causing me to want to pray or need to pray.

2. The Holy Spirit takes the _____ of God and reveals to me the will of God.

3. I pray in the Spirit in _____ with the will of God.

4. I _____ my life to the truth.

5. I look and listen for _____ or further direction from the Bible, circumstances, and the church (other believers).

6. I _____.

7. God works in me and through me to accomplish His purposes.

Has God spoken to you by the Holy Spirit through prayer during this course? Yes ❑ No ❑ If He has, describe below what you sensed He was saying in one of the times He has spoken. If you do not think He has, ask Him to reveal to you the reason.

_____

Has He given you any confirmation through the Bible, circumstances, or the church (other believers)? Yes ❑ No ❑ If so, what did you sense He was saying?

_____

Review today's lesson. Pray and ask God to identify one or more statements or Scriptures that He wants you to understand, learn, or practice. Underline it (them). Then respond to the following:

What was the most meaningful statement or Scripture you read today?

_____

Reword the statement or Scripture into a prayer of response to God.

_____

What does God want you to do in response to today's study?

_____

Review your Scripture memory verses and be prepared to recite them to a partner in your small-group session this week.

SUMMARY STATEMENTS

- When God tells me something important, I should write it down.
- Truth is a Person.
- Prayer is two-way communication with God.
- Prayer is a relationship, not just a religious activity.
- I need to make sure that my only desire is to know God's will.

[1]If you are not keeping a spiritual diary, you may want to use *DiscipleHelps: A Daily Quiet Time Guide and Journal*. It gives brief instructions on how to cultivate a daily quiet time, how to memorize Scripture, how to take sermon notes, and how to use various kinds of prayers. It provides a day-by-day record of your spiritual life. Orders or order inquiries may be sent to Customer Service Center, 127 Ninth Avenue, North, Nashville, TN 37234, or call 1-800-458-BSSB. Order Item 7217-45.

Unit

6

A LIGHTENING BOLT

It was the last day to register for the "Change Your World" youth weekend at the church. Christa was still undecided. On the one hand, she didn't really have the money. And she had a lot of things she had been putting off that she could do that weekend. Besides, she had decided, it was probably going to be another one of those times when everybody got hyped up and made a commitment to something they knew wouldn't last a week.

If I'm really honest with myself, Christa thought, *I would have to say I don't like those weekends.* On the other hand, in the back of her mind, she thought, *Maybe one of these will work.* She knew of a few people whose commitment to God continued after the weekend, and God was really real to them. Like Kendra, her best friend, who always talked about God and encouraged her. In fact, she had given her a quiet-time guide before she went off to college.

Christa had begun to use the quiet-time guide in the mornings, but not very consistently. Her attitude was that she would get up in the morning and see if she felt like having a quiet time. On this particular morning, she decided to take the time, because she needed to make a decision about the weekend. The Scripture selection for this morning was from the Book of Jeremiah.

After finishing her quiet time, Christa knew she had to go ahead and make up her mind. Well, she just wouldn't go. There, she had made the decision. God hadn't hit her with a bolt of lightning during her quiet time to tell her she should go; so that was that.

Then the phone rang. It was Kendra. Through an unusual set of circumstances, Kendra had learned that there was a discipleship weekend going on at the church, and she really felt like God was telling her to pay Christa's way. In fact, she called to tell Christa that she had already paid her way and had registered her.

A lightning bolt, or what! Christa exclaimed silently.

That weekend God spoke to Christa in a special way. She came to the realization that she had learned a lot about God but had never totally surrendered her life to Him. She also realized something else:

> "For I know the plans I have for you," declares the Lord, "plans to prosper you and not to harm you, plans to give you hope and a future. Then you will call upon me and come and pray to me, and I will listen to you" (Jer. 29:11-12).

*Verse to Memorize
This Week*

Jesus gave them this answer: "I tell you the truth, the Son can do nothing by himself; he can do only what he sees his Father doing, because whatever the Father does the Son also does."

—JOHN 5:19

WHAT IS HAPPENING WHEN YOU PRAY?

If I start asking God for one thing and something different happens, I always respond to what begins to happen. I have found that God always has far more to give me than I can even ask or think. Paul said, "Now to him who is able to do immeasurably more than all we ask or imagine, according to his power that is at work within us, to him be glory in the church and in Christ Jesus throughout all generations, for ever and ever!" (Eph. 3:20-21).

You can't even think a prayer that comes close to what God wants to give you. Only the Spirit of God knows what God is doing or purposing in your life. Let God give you all that He wants to give (see 1 Cor. 2:10-12).

 If God wants to give you more than you are asking, would you rather have what you are asking or what God wants to give?

I would rather have _____

Who alone can instruct you in the activity of God in your life?

_____

Spiritual Concentration

Our problem is that we pray and then never relate anything that happens to our praying. After you pray, the greatest single thing you need to do is turn on your spiritual concentration. When you pray in a direction, immediately anticipate the activity of God in answer to your prayer. I find this all the way through the Scripture—when God's people prayed, He responded.

When I pray, I immediately begin to watch for what happens next. I prepare to make adjustments to what begins to happen in my life. When I pray, it never crosses my mind that God is not going to answer. Expect God to answer your prayers, but stick around for the answer. His timing is always right and best.

 Respond to the following:

1. Have you ever prayed persistently for something and did not receive it or gotten something different? Yes ❏ No ❏ Briefly describe one such time.

_____

2. Review what you have just written and make a list of things you can do in response to times like these.

_____

3. Are you praying for anything right now that God is not granting? Yes ❏ No ❏ If so, what are you praying for?

_____

If you answered yes to question 3, ask God to help you understand what He is doing in your life. Then watch to see what happens next, or pay attention to what He begins to reveal to you through His Word.

The Silences of God

I went through a lengthy time when it seemed God was silent. You probably have had that experience, too. I had been praying over many days, and there seemed

Sidebar

Only the Spirit of God knows what God is doing or purposing in my life.

"The Spirit searches all things, even the deep things of God. For who among men knows the thoughts of a man except the man's spirit within him? In the same way no one knows the thoughts of God except the Spirit of God. We have not received the spirit of the world but the Spirit who is from God, that we may understand what God has freely given us."
—1 Corinthians 2:10-12

Our problem is that we pray and then never relate anything that happens to our praying.

Watch to see what happens next.

Expect an answer.

to be total silence from God. I sensed that heaven was shut up. I didn't understand what was happening. Some folk have told me that, if God does not hear my prayer, I have sin in my life. They gave me a "sin checklist" to work through. I prayed through the sin checklist on this occasion. As far as I could tell, I was okay. I could not understand the silence of God.

Job

Do you remember a biblical person who had a problem like this? Job did. His counselors told him that all his problems were because of sin. Job kept saying, "As best I know, God and I are on the right terms." Job did not know all that God was doing during that time, but his counselors were wrong.

 If you have ever had a time when you experienced the silences of God, briefly describe one such time.

_____

The only thing I knew to do was go back to God. I believe that the God who is in a love relationship with me will let me know what is going on in my life when and if I need to know. So I prayed, "Heavenly Father, I don't understand this silence. You are going to have to tell me what You are doing in my life." He did!—from His Word. This became one of the most meaningful experiences in my life.

God will let you know what He is doing in your life when and if you need to know.

I did not frantically go searching for an answer. I continued the daily reading of the Word of God. I was convinced that, as I was reading the Word of God, the Spirit of God (who knew the mind of God for me) was in the process of helping me understand what God was doing in my life. God will let you know what He is doing in your life when and if you need to know.

One morning I was reading the story of the death of Lazarus (John 11:1-45). Let me go through the sequence of what happened as I read. John reported that Jesus loved Lazarus, Mary, and Martha. Having received word that Lazarus was sick unto death, Jesus delayed going to Lazarus' home until he died. In other words, Mary and Martha asked Jesus to come help their brother, and there was silence. All the way through the final sickness and death of Lazarus, Jesus did not respond.

Lazarus

The family went through the entire funeral process. They prepared Lazarus' body for burial, put him in the tomb, and covered the opening with a stone. Still they experienced silence from God. Then Jesus said to His disciples, "Let's go."

When Jesus arrived, Lazarus had been dead four days. Martha said to Jesus, "Lord, if you had been here, my brother would not have died" (v. 32).

Then the Spirit of God began to help me understand something. It seemed to me as if Jesus had said to Mary and Martha:

"You are exactly right. If I had come, your brother would not have died. You know I could have healed him, because you have seen me heal many times. If I had come when you asked me to, I would have healed him. But, you would never have known any more about Me than you already know. I knew you were ready for a greater revelation of Me than you have ever known. I wanted you to come to know that I am the resurrection and the life. My refusal and My silence were not rejection. They were opportunities to disclose more of Me to you."

When that began to dawn on me, I almost jumped straight out of my chair. I said, "That's what's happening in my life! That's what's happening! The silence of

God means He is ready to bring into my life a greater revelation of Himself than I have ever known." With great anticipation, I began to watch for what God was going to teach me about Himself. I then had some things happen in my life that I might never have responded to without that kind of anticipation.

 What are two possible reasons for the silence of God when you pray?

_____

Now, when I pray and there is a silence from God, I still pray through my sin checklist. Sometimes God's silences are due to sin in my life. If there is uncon-fessed sin in my life, I confess it and make it right. If, after that, there is still a silence with God, I get ready for a new experience with God.

You can respond to the silence of God in two ways. One response is for you to go into depression, a sense of guilt, and self-condemnation. The other response is for you to have an expectation that God is about to bring you to a deeper knowledge of Himself. These responses are as different as night and day.

Do you know what set me free? Truth. And, Truth is a Person who is actively involved in my life. The moment I understood what God might have been doing, I made an adjustment of my life to God. I put away the attitude of depression and guilt. I quit feeling that maybe I was of no use to God and that He wouldn't hear me anymore. I made the major adjustment in my life to an attitude of expecta-tion, faith, and trust. The moment I did that, God began to show me how I could respond to Him in such a way that I would know Him in a greater way.

Truth set me free! . . . and Truth is a Person!

 Review today's lesson. Pray and ask God to identify one or more state-ments or Scriptures that He wants you to understand, learn, or prac-tice. Underline it (them). Then respond to the following:

What was the most meaningful statement or Scripture you read today?

_____

Reword the statement or Scripture into a prayer of response to God.

_____

What does God want you to do in response to today's study?

_____

Write your Scripture memory verse for this unit on the following lines and review your verses from other units.

_____

_____

SUMMARY STATEMENTS
- Oh, God, if I ever give You a request and You have more to give me than I am asking, cancel my request.
- Only the Spirit of God knows what God is doing or purposing in my life.
- God will let me know what He is doing in my life when and if I need to know.
- Sometimes God's silences are due to sin.
- Sometimes God is silent as He prepares to bring me into a deeper understanding of Himself.

GOD SPEAKS THROUGH CIRCUMSTANCES

To understand your bad or difficult circumstances, God's perspective is vital.

The Holy Spirit uses the Bible, prayer, and circumstances to speak to us. The role of circumstances in discovering God's will is seen in the way Jesus knew what the Father wanted Him to do. Jesus described the process in John 5:17,19-20.

 Verse 19 is your memory verse this week. Write it below.

_____

_____

"Jesus said to them, 'My Father is always at his work to this very day, and I, too, am working.'"
—John 5:17

Jesus said that He did not take the initiative in what to do for the Father (v. 19). Only the Father has the right to take the initiative. The Father would let the Son know what He was doing (v. 20). When the Son saw the *Father's* activity, that was the Father's invitation for the Son to join Him.

 By way of review, see if you can fill in the blanks in the following sequence, using the key words in the left margin.

Working

Everything

Watch

Father

Doing

Initiative

Loves

1. The _____ has been working right up until now.

2. Now God has Me _____.

3. I do nothing on My own _____.

4. I _____ to see what the Father is doing.

5. I do what I see the Father is already _____.

6. You see, the Father _____ Me.

7. He shows Me _____ that He, Himself, is doing.

Check your answers with the sequence on page 12.

Jesus did not have to guess what to do. Jesus did not have to dream up what He could do for the Father.

The Father loved the Son and showed Him everything He was doing. Jesus watched to see what the Father was doing around His life and put His life there. The Father then could accomplish *His* purposes through Jesus.

This is exactly what Jesus wants us to do with *His* lordship in our lives. We see what He is doing and adjust our lives, our plans, and our goals to *Him*. We are to place our lives at *His* disposal—where He is working—so He can accomplish His purposes through us.

God's Perspective Is Vital

Job

Job did not know what was happening when everything he owned was destroyed, when his children were killed, and when he developed sores all over his body (see Job 1—2). He tried to understand his circumstances. He did not know what was happening from God's perspective (Job 1:6-12; 2:1-7). Neither did He know the last chapter (Job 42:12-17) when God would restore his property, his family, and his health.

Job's friends thought they had God's perspective and told Job to confess his sin. If you didn't have that last chapter and didn't know God's perspective, whose side do you think you would be on? God's or Job's? You probably would be with Job, saying, "I want to ask God what is going on. Why is He allowing this to happen." You would think God was being cruel to Job.

When you face difficult or confusing circumstances, they can overwhelm you. If you put yourself in the middle of the circumstances and try to look at God, you will always have a distorted understanding of God. For instance you might say, "God doesn't love me" or "God is not fair." Both of those statements are false.

 Have you ever been in the middle of a tragic or confusing circumstance when you began to accuse God of things you know are not true of God? Yes ❏ No ❏ If so, describe one of those circumstances.

_____

Perhaps you began to question God's wisdom. Maybe you were afraid to say He was wrong, but you sort of said, "God you deceived me by letting me believe this was the right thing to do. Why didn't you stop me?" A lot of wrong things can happen if you try to look at God from the middle of circumstances.

What do you do? First, ask God to show you His perspective on your circumstance. When you face difficult or confusing circumstances, the Spirit of God again will take the Word of God and help you understand your circumstances from God's perspective. He will reveal to you the truth of the circumstance.

Go to God and ask Him to show you His perspective on your circumstance.

Carrie's Cancer

I told you at the beginning of Unit 3 about our daughter Carrie's bout with cancer. The doctors prepared us for six or eight months of chemotherapy, plus radiation. We knew God loved us, so we went to Him in prayer and asked for understanding about what He was doing or going to do in our lives. We prayed, "What are you purposing to do in this experience that we need to adjust ourselves to?"

"What are you purposing to do in this experience that we need to adjust ourselves to?"

As we prayed, a Scripture promise came that we believed was from God. The verse reads, "This sickness will not end in death. No, it is for God's glory so that God's Son may be glorified through it" (John 11:4). Our sense that God was speaking to us grew stronger as the Bible, prayer, and the testimony of other believers began to say the same thing. We then adjusted our lives to the truth and began to watch for ways God would use this situation for His glory.

During this time, people from Canada, Europe, and the United States began praying for Carrie. One thing surfaced in conversations with many of these people. They said something like this: "Our prayer life (prayer ministry) has become so dry and cold. We haven't seen any special answers to prayer in a long time. But, when we heard about Carrie, we put her on our prayer list."

After *three* months of treatments, the doctors ran more tests. They said, "We don't understand this, but all the tests are negative. We cannot find any trace of the cancer." I began to communicate this answer to prayer with those who were praying for Carrie. In instance after instance people said that this answer to prayer was what God used to totally renew their prayer life.

Then I began to see what God had in mind for this circumstance. Many, many people sensed a fresh call to prayer. They personally began to experience anew the presence of Truth—and Truth as a Person. Some of Carrie's closest friends began to pray fervently at this time. Some students even came to know the Lord after observing what God had done in and through Carrie. God did bring glory to Himself through this sickness.

Do you see what happened? We faced a trying situation. We sought God's perspective. The Holy Spirit took the Word of God and revealed to us God's perspective on the end result of that circumstance. We believed God and adjusted our lives to

Him and to what He was doing. We then went through the circumstance looking for ways His purposes would be accomplished that would bring Him glory. In the process we came to know God in a new way because of the compassion He showed us by revealing His perspective on our situation.

Let me summarize how you can respond when circumstances are confusing:

WHEN CIRCUMSTANCES ARE CONFUSING

1. Settle in your own mind that God has forever demonstrated His absolute love for you on the cross. That love will never change.
2. Go to God and ask Him to help you see His perspective on your situation.
3. Wait on the Holy Spirit to help you understand your circumstances.
4. Adjust your life to God and what you see Him doing in your circumstances.
5. Do all God tells you to do.
6. Experience God working in and through you to accomplish His purposes.

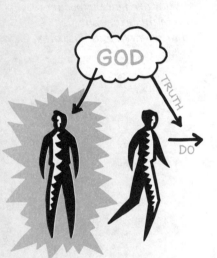

Read again the previous list. Circle a key word or phrase in each statement.

In your own words, summarize what you need to do when you find yourself in circumstances that are confusing.

_____

You do need to remember that God is sovereign. You may face a situation like Job experienced where God does not tell you what He is doing. In those instances acknowledge God's love and sovereignty and depend on His sustaining grace to see you through the situation.

Review today's lesson. Pray and ask God to identify one or more statements or Scriptures that He wants you to understand, learn, or practice. Underline it (them). Then respond to the following:

What was the most meaningful statement or Scripture you read today?

_____

Reword the statement or Scripture into a prayer of response to God.

_____

What does God want you to do in response to today's study?

_____

SUMMARY STATEMENTS

- God used circumstances to reveal to Jesus what He was to do.
- Jesus watched circumstances to know where the Father wanted to involve Him in His work.
- God's perspective is vital in understanding my difficult circumstances.

THE TRUTH OF YOUR CIRCUMSTANCE

You cannot know the truth of your circumstance until you have heard from God. In Exodus 5—6 Moses did as he was told and asked Pharaoh to let Israel go. Pharaoh refused and made life harder for the Israelites. The Israelites criticized Moses for causing so much trouble.

 What would you have done if you had been in Moses' place? Check one or more responses:

❏ 1. I would have gotten mad at Israel and gone back to tending sheep.

❏ 2. I would have gotten mad at God and told Him to get somebody else.

❏ 3. I would have decided that I misunderstood God's will.

❏ 4. I would have patiently gone back to God and asked Him to give me His perspective on this "bad" circumstance.

Moses' story really encourages me. The first three responses are more like the way we usually respond. If you haven't read Exodus 5—6, you may have the idea from what I have said that Moses would have picked response 4. He didn't! He blamed God and accused Him of failing to do what He promised. Moses said, "O Lord, why have you brought trouble upon this people? Is this why you sent me? Ever since I went to Pharaoh to speak in your name, he has brought trouble upon this people, and you have not rescued your people at all" (Ex. 5:22-23). Moses was so discouraged he was ready to quit (Ex. 6:12).

God took time to explain His perspective. He told Moses that He *wanted* Pharaoh to resist so the people could see His mighty hand of deliverance. God wanted the people to know Him (by experience) as the great "I AM." Learn from Moses' example. When you face confusing circumstances, don't start blaming God. Ask Him to reveal the truth of your circumstances.

God is patient.

Hearing from Truth

The disciples were in a boat in a storm. Jesus was asleep in the back of the boat. If you had gone to those disciples and said to them, "What is the truth of this situation?" what would they have said? "We perish!" Was that the truth? No, Truth was asleep at the back of the boat. In just a moment Truth Himself would stand up, and He would stop the storm. Then they knew the Truth of their circumstance. Truth is a person who is always present in your life. You cannot know the truth of your circumstance, until you have heard from God. He is the Truth! And the Truth is present and active in your life!

 Read Luke 7:11-17 at the right and answer the following questions.

1. Before Jesus came, how do you think the widow of Nain would have responded to this question: "What is the truth of this situation?"

   She would have said:_____

2. When Jesus was present, what difference did He make?

   _____

3. When Jesus revealed Himself to the crowd, how did they respond?

   _____

The widow might have said, "My husband died at a young age. I had one son and had anticipated that we would spend wonderful days together. He would care for me, and we would have fellowship together. Now my son is dead, and I must live the rest of my life alone." Was that the truth?

"Jesus went to a town called Nain, and his disciples and a large crowd went along with him. As he approached the town gate, a dead person was being carried out—the only son of his mother, and she was a widow. And a large crowd from the town was with her. When the Lord saw her, his heart went out to her and he said, 'Don't cry.'
Then he went up and touched the coffin, and those carrying it stood still. He said, 'Young man, I say to you, get up!' The dead man sat up and began to talk, and Jesus gave him back to his mother.
They were all filled with awe and praised God. 'A great prophet has appeared among us,' they said. 'God has come to help his people.' This news about Jesus spread throughout Judea and the surrounding country."

—Luke 7:11-17

You never know the truth of any situation until you have heard from Jesus.

No, Truth was standing there! When Truth reached out and touched her son and restored him, all was changed. You never know the truth of any situation until you have heard from Jesus. When Jesus was allowed to reveal Himself in this circumstance, the people "were all filled with awe and praised God. 'A great prophet has appeared among us,' they said. 'God has come to help his people'" (Luke 7:16). Never, ever determine the truth of a situation by looking at the circumstances. Don't evaluate your situation until you have heard from Jesus.

 Read John 6:1-15 and answer the following questions.

1. Five thousand hungry people came to Jesus. He wanted to feed them. If you had asked the disciples what the truth of the situation was, how do you think they would have responded?

_____

2. Why did Jesus ask Philip where they could buy bread? (vv. 5-6)

_____

3. When Truth (Jesus) was present what difference did it make?

_____

4. When Truth (Jesus) revealed Himself to that crowd, how did they respond? (v. 14)

_____

Can you trust Him with the other half of the story?

I wonder if God ever tests our faith like He did Philip's. Does He say, "Feed the multitudes," and our church responds, "Our budget couldn't do it"? If you had asked the disciples at that moment about the truth of the situation, they may have said, "We can't do it. Lord. It is impossible." Was that true? No. We know the other half of the story. Wouldn't we be better off if we trusted God with the other half of the story in our lives?

Suppose God says to your church, "Take the gospel to the whole world!" and the group says, "We can't." Truth stands in the middle of that church to say, "Believe Me. I will never give you an order that I will not Myself release My power to enable it to happen. Trust Me and obey Me, and it will happen."

 Review today's lesson. Pray and ask God to identify one or more statements or Scriptures that He wants you to understand, learn, or practice. Underline it (them). Then respond to the following:

What was the most meaningful statement or Scripture you read today?

_____

Reword the statement or Scripture into a prayer of response to God.

_____

What does God want you to do in response to today's study?

_____

SUMMARY STATEMENTS

• Never determine the truth of a situation by looking at the circumstances.
• I cannot know the truth of my circumstance, until I have heard from God.
• The Holy Spirit reveals God's perspective on the circumstance.

SPIRITUAL MARKERS

The discussion about circumstances on the first two days of this unit may imply that a circumstance is a bad situation. That is not always the case. Sometimes a circumstance is a decision-making situation. In a decision-making time, your greatest difficulty may not be choosing between good and bad but choosing between good and best. Often, you may have several options that all appear to be good. At a time like this, the place to start is to say with all of your heart:

> "Lord, whatever I know to be Your will, I will do it. Regardless of the cost and regardless of the adjustment, as best I know my heart, I commit myself to follow Your will ahead of time. Lord, no matter what Your will looks like, I will do it!"

You need to say that at the beginning of seeking God's will. Otherwise you do not mean, "Thy will be done." You would be saying, "Thy will be done as long as it does not conflict with my will." Two words in the Christian's language cannot go together: *No, Lord*. If you say, "No," He is not Lord. If He really is your Lord, your answer must always be "Yes." In decision making, always begin here. Do not proceed until you can honestly say, "Whatever you want of me, Lord, I will do it."

When God gets ready for you to take a new step or direction in His activity, it will always be in sequence with what He has already been doing in your life.

"Yes, Lord!"

Physical Markers of Spiritual Encounters

When Israel crossed the Jordan River into the promised land, God gave Joshua the following instructions: "Choose twelve men from among the people, one from each tribe, and tell them to take up twelve stones from the middle of the Jordan from right where the priests stood and to carry them over with you and put them down at the place where you stay tonight" (Josh. 4:2-3). These stones were to serve as a sign to the Israelites, "a memorial to the people of Israel forever" (see Josh. 4:6-7). The stones were to be a reminder of a mighty act of God in behalf of His people.

These stones will serve as a sign to you.

Select ONE of the following persons. Check the box beside the person you choose to study. Read about his encounter with God. Then answer the questions that follow.

- ❏ **Noah**–Genesis 6–8
- ❏ **Abram**–Genesis 12:1-8 or 13:1-18
- ❏ **Isaac**–Genesis 26:17-25
- ❏ **Jacob**–Genesis 28:10-22 and 35:1-7
- ❏ **Moses**–Exodus 17:8-16 or 24:1-11
- ❏ **Joshua**–Joshua 3:5–4:9
- ❏ **Gideon**–Judges 6:11-24
- ❏ **Samuel**–1 Samuel 7:1-13

1. Describe the encounter between the person and God. What did God do?

_____

_____

2. Why do you think the person built an altar or set up the stone marker?

_____

3. What, if any, special names of God or of the stone/altar are given?

_____

THE LORD HELPED ME

On many other occasions people built altars or set up stones as reminders of their encounters with God. Places like Bethel ("house of God") and Rehoboth ("room") became reminders of God's great activity in the midst of His people. Moses named an altar "The Lord is my Banner" (Ex. 17:15), and Samuel named a stone

These altars and stones became physical markers of great spiritual encounters with God.

"Ebenezer" saying, "Thus far has the Lord helped us" (1 Sam. 7:12). These altars and stones became physical markers of great spiritual encounters with God. They provided an opportunity for people to teach their children about the activity of God in behalf of His people.

Seeing God's Perspective

God works in sequence to accomplish His divine purposes. What He did in the past was done with a Kingdom purpose in mind. What He is doing in the present is in sequence with the past and with the same Kingdom purpose in mind. Every act of God builds on the past with a view toward the future.

God gave perspective on what He was doing.

When God called Abraham (Gen. 12), He began to develop a people for Himself. When God came to Isaac, He reminded Isaac of His relationship with Isaac's father Abraham (Gen. 26:24). To Jacob God identified Himself as the God of Abraham and Isaac (Gen. 28:13). When God came to Moses, He helped Moses see His perspective of what He was doing through history. He said He was the God of Abraham, Isaac, and Jacob (Ex. 3:6-10). At each new step in His divine plan, God involved a person.

Moses gave perspective on what God was doing.

Israel needed to see that the new direction was in line with all that God had been doing.

God wanted His people to have the perspective of history as they took a new step. In Deuteronomy 29 Moses gave a brief summary of the nation's history. At this time of covenant renewal, Moses wanted to remind the people to be faithful in following God. They were getting ready to change leaders (from Moses to Joshua) and move into the promised land. They needed to see this new direction from God's perspective. Israel needed to see that the new direction was in line with all that God had been doing.

Moses

Look at the perspective God gave Moses when He called him into service at the burning bush in Exodus 3. In the lines that follow:

- Write PAST beside items that speak of God's past activity with His people.
- Write PRESENT beside those items that speak of what God was doing at the time He spoke to Moses.
- Write FUTURE beside items that speak of what God was going to do.

_____ 1. "I am the God of your father, the God of Abraham, the God of Isaac and the God of Jacob" (v.6).

_____ 2. "I have indeed seen the misery of my people in Egypt. I have heard them crying out because of their slave drivers" (v. 7).

_____ 3. "I am concerned about their suffering. So I have come down to rescue them from the hand of the Egyptians" (vv. 7-8).

_____ 4. "So now, go. I am sending you to Pharaoh to bring my people the Israelites out of Egypt" (v. 10).

_____ 5. "I will be with you. And this will be the sign to you that it is I who have sent you: When you have brought the people out of Egypt, you will worship God on this mountain" (v. 12).

_____ 6. "I have promised to bring you up out of your misery in Egypt into the land of the Canaanites . . . a land flowing with milk and honey" (v. 17).

_____ 7. "I will make the Egyptians favorably disposed toward this people, so that when you leave you will not go empty-handed" (v. 21).

Items 1, 2, and 6 are past. Items 3 and 4 are present. Items 5 and 7 are future.

Do you see what God was doing with Moses? He was helping Moses see his call from God's perspective.

- God had been working with Abraham, Isaac, Jacob, and even Moses' father to build a nation.
- God had promised Abraham that He would bring the people out of bondage and give them the promised land.
- God had been watching over them in Egypt.
- Now God was ready to respond to the suffering of His people.
- God had chosen to involve Moses in His divine purpose for Israel. He was going to use Moses to deliver the Israelites out of Egypt.
- After Moses obeyed, God would bring them to this mountain to worship. The worship service on the mountain would be Moses' sign that God had sent him.

God wants to involve you in His purposes. He has been working in the world all along (John 5:17). He has been working in your life since your birth. He was working out His purposes for your life prior to your birth. God said to Jeremiah the prophet, "Before I formed you in the womb I knew you, before you were born I set you apart; I appointed you as a prophet to the nations" (Jer. 1:5). When God gets ready for you to take a new step or direction in His activity, it will always be in sequence with what He already has been doing in your life. He builds your character in an orderly fashion with a divine purpose in mind.

A Spiritual Inventory

One thing I have found helpful is to identify "spiritual markers" in my life. Each time I have encountered God's call or directions for my life, I have mentally built a spiritual marker at that point. A spiritual marker identifies a time of transition, decision, or direction when I clearly know that God has guided me. I can look back at these spiritual markers and see how God has faithfully directed my life according to His divine purpose.

A spiritual marker identifies a time of transition, decision, or direction when I clearly know that God has guided me.

When I face a decision about God's direction, I rehearse those spiritual markers. I don't take the next step without the context of the full activity of God in my life. This helps me see God's perspective for my past and present. Then I look at the options that are before me. I look to see which one of the options seems to be most consistent with what God has been doing in my life. Often one of these directions will be most consistent with what God already has been doing. If none of the directions seem consistent, I continue to pray and wait on the Lord's guidance. When circumstances do not align with what God is saying in the Bible and in prayer, I assume that the timing may be wrong. I then wait for God to reveal His timing.

Using spiritual markers

 In your own words write a definition of "spiritual markers."

_____

Using the previous paragraph, describe in your own words how you could use spiritual markers to help you determine God's direction at a time of decision.

_____

_____

Why do you think "spiritual markers" are helpful? What do they help you do?

_____

_____

My call to the Home Mission Board

In 1988 Bob Hamblin from the Home Mission Board called me. He said, "Henry, we have prayed much about filling a position in prayer for spiritual awakening. We have been seeking a person for over two years to fill this position. Would you consider coming and directing Southern Baptists in the area of spiritual awakening?"

"Spiritual awakening has been a deep current through my life."

As I reviewed God's activity in my life (my spiritual markers), I saw that an emphasis on spiritual awakening was an important element throughout my ministry. I said to Bob, "You could have asked me to do anything in the world, and I would not have even prayed about leaving Canada—except spiritual awakening. That has been a deep current running through my life since the time I was an older teenager, and more particularly since 1958." After much prayer and confirmation in the Word and by other believers, I accepted the position at the Home Mission Board. God didn't shift me, He focused me in something He already had been doing down the course of my life.

 Prepare a spiritual inventory of your life. Identify your own spiritual markers. These may begin with your heritage, your salvation experience, times you made significant decisions regarding your future, and so forth. What are some of the times of transition, decision, or direction in your life when you knew clearly that God guided you? Using a separate sheet of paper or a notebook start preparing a list. Start this list today, but don't feel that you have to have a complete list. Add to it as you reflect and pray about God's activity in your life.

You will have opportunity to share some of your spiritual markers in this week's small-group session.

 Review today's lesson. Pray and ask God to identify one or more statements or Scriptures that He wants you to understand, learn, or practice. Underline it (them). Then respond to the following:

What was the most meaningful statement or Scripture you read today?

_____

Reword the statement or Scripture into a prayer of response to God.

_____

_____

What does God want you to do in response to today's study?

_____

SUMMARY STATEMENTS

- In a decision-making time my greatest difficulty may not be choosing between good and bad, but choosing between good and best.
- Two words in the Christian's language cannot go together: *No, Lord.*
- God works in sequence to accomplish His divine purposes.
- When God gets ready for me to take a new step or direction in His activity, it will be in sequence with what He has already been doing in my life.
- A spiritual marker identifies a time of transition, decision, or direction when I clearly know that God has guided me.

GOD SPEAKS THROUGH THE CHURCH

DAY

5

The Holy Spirit speaks to us through God's people, the local church. Today we will look at ways to help you understand God's will through the church.

As I function in relationship to the church, I depend on others in the church to help me understand God's will.

 Let's review for a moment. Answer the following questions.

1. How did God speak in the Old Testament?

_____

2. How did God speak in the Gospels?

_____

3. How does God speak from Acts through the present?

_____

4. What are four ways the Holy Spirit speaks to Christians?

_____

The Body of Christ

A church is a body. It is the body of Christ (1 Cor. 12:27)! Jesus Christ is Head of a local church (Eph. 4:15), and every member is placed in the body as it pleases God (1 Cor. 12:18). The whole body is fitted together by the Father. The Holy Spirit gives gifts to members of the body to be used "for the common good" (1 Cor. 12:7). Members are enabled and equipped by the Holy Spirit to function where the Father has placed them in the body. God made us mutually interdependent. We need one another. What one lacks, others in the body can and will supply.

Therefore, what God is doing in and through the body is essential to my knowing how to respond to Him. In the church, I let God use me in any way He chooses to complete His work in each member. This was Paul's goal when he said, "We proclaim him, admonishing and teaching everyone with all wisdom, so that we may present everyone perfect in Christ" (Col. 1:28). Paul was constantly asking the believers to become involved with his life and ministry. The effectiveness of Paul's ministry rested on them (see 2 Thess. 3:1; Eph. 6:19).

"Instead, speaking the truth in love, we will in all things grow up into him who is the Head, that is, Christ. From him the whole body, joined and held together by every supporting ligament, grows and builds itself up in love, as each part does its work."
—Ephesians 4:15-16

 Read 1 Corinthians 12:7-31 and answer the following questions.

1. Paul was addressing the Christians of a local church, the church of Corinth. What is a local church? (v. 27)

_____

2. Based on verse 12, circle one of the following pictures that best illustrates a church.

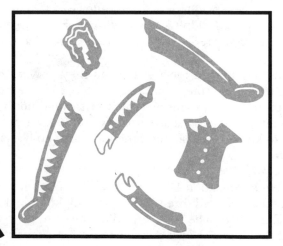

A

B

UNIT 6 · **101**

3. What does verse 25 say should be true of the church? Is this true of your church?

_____

4. Based on verses 14-24, mark the statements below as T (true) or F (false). For the statements that are false, rewrite the statement on the line provided, so that it is stated correctly.

_____ a. The body is made up of one part.

_____

_____ b. The foot is still a part of the body, even though it is not a hand.

_____

_____ c. The ear is not part of the body, because it is not an eye.

_____

_____ d. Members of the body decide how they should be arranged.

_____

_____ e. All the members need every other member of the body.

_____

Answers: (1) A local church is the body of Christ. All believers worldwide are united in the kingdom of God under the rule of the King! But the local church is to function like a body. It is not *part* of a body. It *is* a body. (2) Picture A may better represent the way some churches function. However, God has always intended for the church to function as a unit, not just as individual parts. (3) The church should have no division in the body. If your church does have division, it is a sick body of Christ. The Great Physician, Christ Himself, can bring about healing of the body, if your church will let Him. (4) Statements a, c, and d are false. The others are true.

Apart from the body, you cannot fully know God's will for your relationship to the body. As I function in relationship to the church, I depend on others in the church to help me understand God's will. In the following paragraphs, I will illustrate this for you.

Allow God to Speak Through the Church

While I was in seminary, I was involved in a local church. The first year I taught a group of youth. I did that with a willing heart. The next year I was asked to be music and education director. I had never done that in my life. I had sung in a choir, but I had never led a bit of music. I didn't know anything about directing the educational program of this church. Here is how I approached this decision.

The people of God at this church had a need for a leader. As they prayed they sensed that God put me there purposely to meet that need. I, too, saw the need and realized God could use me there. As a servant of Jesus Christ, I did not have an option to say no. I believed that the Head—Jesus Christ—could speak through the rest of the body to guide me to know how I should function in the body. I said I would do the best I knew to do.

For two years I served as Music and Education Director. Then the church voted to call me to be their pastor. I hadn't preached three sermons in my life. I had not gone to the seminary because I felt called to be a pastor. I did, however, go to the seminary because I felt called of God into a *relationship* with Him for *whatever* He had in mind. I sensed that I needed to put the seminary training in place, so that I would have some tools for God to work with. I didn't say, "I am going into foreign missions or home missions." I didn't say music, or education, or preaching. I said, "Lord, whatever You direct me to do in relation to your body, that is what I will do. I am your servant." So, I agreed to be their pastor.

Don't ever be afraid to let the body of believers assist you in knowing God's will. Keep in mind, also, that one individual is not the church. In the final analysis, you are going to have to take all the counsel of people and go to God for the clear direction. What you will find is that a number of things begin to line up. What you are hearing from the Bible and prayer and circumstances and the church will begin to say the same thing. Then you can proceed with confidence.

You may say to me, "Henry, you don't know my church. I can't depend on them to help me know God's will." Be careful. When you say that, you have said more about what you believe about God than what you believe about your church. You are saying, "Henry, not even God can work through these people. He just is not powerful enough." You don't believe that in your mind, I don't think. But what you do says more about what you believe about God than what you say.

"Henry, you don't know my church."

This is the point where we need to focus on the *crisis of belief*. Watch out! Next week may be a real challenge to you.

 Review today's lesson. Pray and ask God to identify one or more statements or Scriptures that He wants you to understand, learn, or practice. Underline it (them). Then respond to the following:

What was the most meaningful statement or Scripture you read today?

_____

Reword the statement or Scripture into a prayer of response to God.

_____

What does God want you to do in response to today's study?

_____

Review your Scripture memory verses and be prepared to recite them to a partner in your small-group session this week.

If you have not completed your list of spiritual markers (Day 4), try to finish before your group session this week. Bring the paper or notebook with you to the session.

SUMMARY STATEMENTS

- A church is a body. It is the body of Christ!
- Jesus Christ is present as Head of a local church.
- Every member is placed in the body as it pleases God.
- God made us mutually interdependent. We need one another.
- Apart from the body, I cannot fully know God's will for my relationship to the body.
- Every member needs to be listening to what the other members are saying.
- As I function in relationship to the church, I depend on others in the church to help me understand God's will.

THE CRISIS OF BELIEF

Unit

SCARED TO DEATH

The meeting of the Christian Students Organization was really exciting. Everyone left the meeting "pumped up." Several members had pledged to witness to at least one other person on the way home. Although Tom, the president, and two of his friends felt God convicting them to follow through on their commitment, they were scared to death! But they were determined.

Tom and his friends stopped at a convenience store and approached the first two men they saw inside. They introduced themselves and asked the men if they knew Jesus. They didn't want to hear about Jesus.

The man behind the counter, who was looking on, remarked, "I know a lot about Jesus."

"Knowing *about* Jesus isn't the most important thing," Tom told him. "What's most important is that you really know Jesus."

Tom's statement made the man uncomfortable. So, needless to say, the conversation went downhill from there. The three youth left the store feeling disappointed but not defeated. They decided to try again. This time they stopped at a supermarket. Although it was closed, three men were still working outside. Two of the men told Tom and his friends that, if they wanted to talk to anyone about Jesus, they should talk with the other guy, who happened to be a preacher.

"You're going about it all wrong," the preacher told them, then criticized them for witnessing that way. Tom wondered if they had done the right thing.

Five years later Tom got his answer. Walking into the music building of the university he was attending, he was approached by a very clean-cut, middle-aged man. The man asked if his name was Tom. When Tom said that it was, the man excitedly introduced himself as Earl and said that he was the chaplain of the state correctional institute. He told Tom that their first meeting made a lasting effect on his life.

Earl was the cashier in the convenience store. That night, five years earlier, he went home, got on his knees, and prayed to receive Christ. Since that time many people have come to know Christ through his ministry.

Through that experience, Tom learned what a simple act of obedience could do in the hands of God—even when you're scared to death.

Verse to Memorize This Week

Without faith it is impossible to please God, because anyone who comes to him must believe that he exists and that he rewards those who earnestly seek him.

—HEBREWS 11:6

A TURNING POINT

This unit focuses on a turning point in your following God's will. When God invites you to join Him in His work, He has a God-sized assignment for you. You will realize that you cannot do it on your own. If God doesn't help you, you will fail. This is the crisis point where many decide not to follow what they sense God is leading them to do. Then they wonder why they do not experience God's presence and activity the way other Christians do.

Let's spend a few minutes reviewing the relationship between the crisis of belief and what you have already studied.

 We have been studying seven realities of the sequence in which God works with His people. Using the following hints, see if you can write the first four in your own words. Then check yourself on the inside back cover of the book.

1. God's work _____

2. Relationship _____

3. Invites _____

4. Speaks _____

Now, see if you can fill in the blanks in the fifth reality. You can peek, if you must.

5. God's invitation for you to work with Him always leads you to a _____

of _____ that requires _____ and _____ .

Crisis

The word *crisis* comes from a word that means "decision." The same Greek word is often translated *judgment*. The crisis of belief is a turning point when you must make a decision. You must decide what you believe about God. How you respond at this turning point will determine whether you go on to be involved with God in something God-sized that only He can do, or whether you will continue to go your own way and miss what God has purposed for your life. This is not a one-time experience. It is a daily experience. How you live your life is a testimony of what you believe about God.

 You learned about Tom at the beginning of this unit. In that experience, what was the crisis of belief? Check your response.

❏ 1. When they decided to go out and witness that evening.
❏ 2. When they decided to go to the supermarket after being discouraged at the convenience store.
❏ 3. When Earl accepted Christ.

In a way, you could have checked all three choices. In each case the persons involved had to decide what they believed about God. Tom and his friends had to decide if they feared witnessing more than they trusted God's power to work through them. After the rejection they experienced at the convenience store, another step of faith was necessary to move on to the supermarket.

The greatest crisis of belief that evening was for Earl, who had to decide what he believed about God. Could God save him? Could God change him? Earl believed God could. His response to that crisis of belief has had a monumental impact on the kingdom of God. If Tom had decided he was too afraid to witness that evening, many people, whose lives Earl touched, might never have come to know Christ. And we would have missed seeing what God could do through that one man.

A. In your own words, define "crisis of belief."

_____

_____

B. Read each of the following passages of Scripture and describe the crisis of belief you see in each situation.

Joshua 6:1-5, 20 _____

_____

Judges 6:33; 7:1-8 _____

_____

_____

1 Chronicles 14:8-16 _____

_____

Matthew 17:24-27 _____

_____

C. Have you or your church ever sensed that God wanted you to do something big, and you faced a crisis of belief? Yes ❑ No ❑ If so, describe one situation and how you (or your church) responded.

_____

_____

_____

D. What did your response demonstrate about your belief in God? Did it show faith or lack of faith?

_____

_____

Joshua and the walls of Jericho

Would you tell an entire army to march with you around a walled city, expecting the walls to fall down when you blow some trumpets? That was a crisis of belief for Joshua and for all Israel as well. They had to decide if they believed God could do what He said. Even though this group had just seen God dam up the Jordan River for them to cross, this next step still required faith. In fact, every assignment God gave Israel required a new measure of faith.

Gideon and his 300 men

Gideon really must have struggled with his crisis. Joint forces of the Midianites, Amalekites, and other Eastern peoples were prepared to attack. Gideon started with 32,000 men, but God had Gideon send 31,700 of them home. He was going to give victory with 300. Do you see what a difference it made from God's perspective? When the battle was won, everyone knew God did it!

David and the Philistines

David refused to rely on human wisdom for guidance. He asked for God's direction. Was this a crisis of belief, since God said He would give David victory over the Philistines? Yes! David still had to decide what he believed about God. He had to trust God to do what He said He would do.

Did you notice that David stayed in a close relationship with God. He didn't depend on yesterday's guidance for today's decision. He didn't use human wisdom to decide whether to attack a second time. This is a good example of how God wants you to depend on Him. What worked yesterday may not be what God wants to use today. Only He has a right to tell you what to do next!

Peter was a fisherman. Never before had he found coins in the mouth of a fish. Great faith was required to go and catch one fish to find the exact amount for the tax! He acted on his faith, and God provided.

Peter, a fish, and taxes

As we continue our study of the crisis of belief, we will examine four principles. These are:

THE CRISIS OF BELIEF

1. An encounter with God requires faith.
2. Encounters with God are God-sized.
3. What you do in response to God's revelation (invitation) reveals what you believe about God.
4. True faith requires action.

 In the previous list, underline a key word or phrase in each principle.

Review today's lesson. Pray and ask God to identify one or more statements or Scriptures that He wants you to understand, learn, or practice. Underline it (them). Then respond to the following.

What was the most meaningful statement or Scripture you read today?

_____

Reword the statement or Scripture into a prayer of response to God.

_____

_____

What does God want you to do in response to today's study?

_____

Write your Scripture memory verse for this unit on the following lines, and review your verses from other units.

_____

_____

_____

SUMMARY STATEMENTS

• When God invites me to join Him in His work, He has a God-sized assignment for me.
• How I live my life is a testimony of what I believe about God.
• When God tells me what He wants to do through me, I will face a crisis of belief.

DAY 2

ENCOUNTERS WITH GOD REQUIRE FAITH

Faith is confidence that what God has promised or said will happen.

When God speaks, your response requires faith. Throughout Scripture, when God revealed Himself and His purposes, the response to Him required faith.

 Read the following Scriptures and respond to the questions.

1. "Faith is being sure of what we hope for and certain of what we do not see" (Heb. 11:1). **What is "faith"?**

_____

2. "We live by faith, not by sight" (2 Cor. 5:7). **What is an opposite of faith?**

_____

3. Jesus said, "Anyone who has faith in me will do what I have been doing. He will do even greater things than these, because I am going to the Father" (John 14:12). **What is the potential of faith?**

_____

4. "If you have faith as small as a mustard seed, you can say to this mountain, 'Move from here to there' and it will move. Nothing will be impossible for you" (Matt. 17:20-21). **How much faith is required for God to do through you what is humanly impossible?**

_____

5. Paul said, "My message and my preaching were not with wise and persuasive words, but with a demonstration of the Spirit's power, so that your faith might not rest on men's wisdom, but on God's power" (1 Cor. 2:4-5). **On what should we base our faith? On what should we NOT base our faith?**

We should base our faith on _____

We should not base our faith on _____

6. "If you do not stand firm in your faith, you will not stand at all" (Isa. 7:9). **What is one danger of lack of faith?**

_____

Faith is confidence that what God has promised or said will happen. Sight is an opposite of faith. If you can see clearly how something can be accomplished, more than likely faith is not required. Remember Tom's experience? If he had chosen to operate on what he knew he could do, faith would not have been necessary.

> Faith is believing that the God who calls us to assignments is the One who will provide for their accomplishment.

Faith is in a Person.

Your faith does not rest in an idea. Faith must be in a PERSON—God Himself. If you decide that it would be nice for some particular thing to happen; and then you lead other people to "believe" or "have faith," you are in a dangerous position. Faith is only valid in God and what He says He is purposing to do.

Jesus said His followers would do even greater things than He had done. With only a mustard-seed (very small) size faith in God, nothing is impossible (see Matt. 17:20). Our faith, however, must be based on God's power and not on human wisdom. Without a firm faith, you will stumble and fall.

Something Only God Can Do

Moses

Moses could not deliver Israel from Pharaoh's army, cross the Red Sea on dry land, provide water from a rock, or provide food. Moses had to have faith that the God who called him would do the things He said He would do.

The disciples

This was also true for Jesus' disciples. On their own, they could not feed the multitudes, heal the sick, stop a storm, or raise the dead. Only God could do these things. God called servants to let Him do these things through them.

When God lets you know what He wants to do through you, it will be something only He can do. If you have faith in the God who called you, you will obey Him; and He will bring to pass what He has purposed to do. If you lack faith, you will not do what He wants. That is disobedience. Jesus asked those around Him, "Why do you call me, 'Lord, Lord,' and do not do what I say?" (Luke 6:46).

 Answer the following questions:

1. What are some things God wanted to do through Moses that only God could do?

_____

_____

2. What are some things Jesus wanted to do through the disciples that only God could do?

_____

_____

3. When God asks a person to join Him in doing something only He can do, what is required for the person to respond?

_____

4. If the person disobeys God, what does that indicate?

_____

5. If the person obeys, what does that indicate?

_____

6. Your memory verse (Heb. 11:6) tells why faith is important. **Write it here:**

_____

_____

Obedience shows faith

When God calls a person to join Him in a God-sized task, faith is required. Obedience indicates faith in God. Disobedience often indicates lack of faith. Without faith, one cannot please God. Without faith, a church cannot please God.

God reveals what He is going to do through us.

Christians today face the same crisis of faith that Bible personalities faced. When God speaks, what He asks of us requires faith. Our major problem, however, is our self-centeredness. We think we have to accomplish the assignment in our own power. We think, "I can't do that. That is not possible." We forget that, when God speaks, He always reveals what *He* is going to do. We join Him so He can do His work through us. We don't have to be able to accomplish the task within our limited ability or resources. With faith, we can proceed confidently to obey God; because we know He is going to bring to pass what He purposes.

"Jesus looked at them and said, 'With man this is impossible, but not with God; all things are possible with God.' "

—Mark 10:27

Describe a time in your life that required faith in God, and you did not respond because you lacked faith.

_____

_____

Describe a time in your life that required faith in God and you responded in faith. (If, after some thought, you cannot think of a time, do not make one up just for the sake of a response.)

_____

_____

What is God wanting you to do right now that you are not doing?

_____

Why do you think you are hesitating?

_____

Have you ever wanted to pray like the disciples when they asked the Lord, "Increase our faith" (Luke 17:5)? Yes ❑ No ❑

Right now, take a few moments to pray about your FAITH and what God is wanting to do through your life.

Review today's lesson. Pray and ask God to identify one or more statements or Scriptures that He wants you to understand, learn, or practice. Underline it (them). Then respond to the following:

What was the most meaningful statement or Scripture you read today?

_____

Reword the statement or Scripture into a prayer of response to God.

_____

_____

What does God want you to do in response to today's study?

_____

_____

SUMMARY STATEMENTS

- When God speaks, my response requires faith.
- Faith is confidence that what God has promised or said will happen.
- Sight is an opposite of faith.
- Faith must be in a Person.
- Before I call myself, my family, or my church to exercise faith, I must be sure I have heard a word from God.
- When God lets me know what He wants to do through me, it will be something only God can do.
- What I believe about God will determine what I do.

ENCOUNTERS WITH GOD ARE GOD-SIZED

God is interested in the world's coming to know Him. The only way people will know what God is like is when they see Him at work. They know His nature when they see His nature expressed in His activity. Whenever God involves you in His activity, the assignment will have God-like dimensions to it.

God is interested in the world's coming to know Him.

God-sized Assignments

The kind of assignments God gives in the Bible are always God-sized. They are always beyond what people can do, because He wants to demonstrate His nature, His strength, His provision, and His kindness to His people and to a watching world. That is the only way the world will come to know Him.

The kind of assignments God gives are God-sized.

 From memory, list some assignments God (either the Father or Jesus) gave to people in the Bible that were "God-sized" assignments—things that were humanly impossible.

_____

_____

You could name many God-sized assignments in Scripture. God told Abraham to father a nation when Abraham had no son and Sarah was past the age to bear children. He told Moses to deliver the children of Israel. He told Gideon to defeat the giant Midianite army with 300 men. Jesus told the disciples to feed the multitudes and to make disciples of all the nations. None of these things were humanly possible. When God's people and the world see something happen that only God can do, they come to know God.

People Come to Know God

 Read the following biblical accounts of God's activity through His servants. Underline statements that indicate how people responded to God's activity when they observed it. I have underlined one for you.

God had Moses lead the Israelites to camp beside the Red Sea. God knew He was going to deliver them by dividing the sea. God said, "I will gain glory for myself through Pharaoh and all his army, and the Egyptians will know that I am the Lord" (Ex. 14:4). What was the result? "When the Israelites saw the great power the Lord displayed against the Egyptians, <u>the people feared the Lord and put their trust in him</u>" (Ex. 14:31).

Moses and the Red Sea

God commanded Joshua to lead the Israelites across the Jordan River at flood stage. Why? "He did this so that all the peoples of the earth might know that the hand of the Lord is powerful and so that you [Israel] might always fear the Lord your God" (Josh. 4:24).

Joshua and the Jordan River

Shadrach, Meshach, and Abednego chose to obey God rather than King Nebuchadnezzar. Before being thrown into a blazing furnace, they said, "The God we serve is able to save us from it, and he will rescue us from your hand" (Dan. 3:17). The soldiers standing by died, but God delivered these three faithful men.

Shadrach, Meshach, and Abednego

King Nebuchadnezzar said, "Praise be to the God of Shadrach, Meshach and Abednego, who has sent his angel and rescued his servants" (Dan. 3:28). And this pagan king wrote these words to the whole nation: "It is my pleasure to tell you about the miraculous signs and wonders that the Most High God has performed for me. How great are his signs, how mighty his wonders!" (Dan. 4:2-3).

The early church

The disciples were filled with the Holy Spirit and spoke in foreign languages that they had not learned. Then Peter preached and "Those who accepted his message were baptized, and about three thousand were added to their number that day" (Acts 2:41).

God used Peter to raise Dorcas from the dead. "This became known all over Joppa, and many people believed in the Lord" (Acts 9:42).

Answer the following questions.

1. When people saw God at work through His servants, who got the credit—God or the servants?

_____

2. What difference or impact do you see in the lives of people who saw or heard about God's activity?

_____

3. How would you describe the response of the people in your community to the gospel of Jesus Christ?

_____

Let the world see God at work and that will attract people!

Our world is not attracted to the Christ we serve, because they cannot see Him at work. They see us doing good things for God and say, "That is wonderful, but that is not my thing." The world is passing us by, because they do not want to get involved in what they see. They are not having an opportunity to see God. Let the world see God at work and He will attract people to Himself. Let Christ be lifted up—not in words, but in life. Let them see the difference that a living Christ makes in a life, a family, or a church; that will make a difference in how they respond. When the world sees things happening through God's people that cannot be explained except that God Himself has done them, then the world will be drawn to the God they see.

 Answer the following questions.

1. How will the world come to know God?

_____

2. Why are people in our world not being attracted to Christ and His church?

_____

3. What kinds of assignments does God give His people?

_____

4. Why does God give God-sized assignments that the individual or church cannot do on their own?

_____

5. What are you attempting to do that only God can make happen?

_____

6. What is your church attempting to do that only God can make happen?

_____

7. Which of the following *best* describes the things you listed in questions 5 and 6? **Check your response.**

❑ a. They are things God led me/us to attempt.

❑ b. They are things I/we decided would be challenging to ask God to do.

8. What connection do you see between people's response to the gospel and the kinds of things you attempt that are God-sized?

❑ a. We are not attempting many God-sized tasks, and few people are responding to the gospel.

❑ b. We are not attempting many God-sized tasks, but many are responding to the gospel.

❑ c. We are seeing God do great things in and through our church, but few people are responding to the gospel.

❑ d. We are seeing God do great things in and through our church, and many people are responding to the gospel.

The world comes to know God when they see God's nature expressed through His activity. When God starts to work, He accomplishes something only He can do. When God does that, both God's people and the world come to know Him in ways they have never known Him before. That is why God gives God-sized assignments to His people. The reason much of the world is not being attracted to Christ and His church is that God's people lack the faith to attempt those things that only God can do. If you or your church are not responding to God and attempting things that only He can accomplish, then you are not exercising faith. "Without faith it is impossible to please God" (Heb. 11:6).

God is far more interested in your having an experience with Him, than He is interested in getting a job done. You can complete a job and never experience God at all. What is He interested in? You and the world—knowing Him and experiencing Him.

You will rejoice that you have experienced Him.

 Review today's lesson. Pray and ask God to identify one or more statements or Scriptures that He wants you to understand, learn, or practice. Underline it (them). Then respond to the following:

What was the most meaningful statement or Scripture you read today?

_____

Reword the statement or Scripture into a prayer of response to God.

_____

What does God want you to do in response to today's study?

_____

SUMMARY STATEMENTS

- The kind of assignments God gives are God-sized.
- When God's people and the world see something only God can do, they come to know God.
- Let people see the difference that a living Christ makes in a life, a family, or a church; that will make a difference in how they respond to the gospel.

DAY 4

WHAT YOU DO TELLS WHAT YOU BELIEVE

What you do reveals what you believe about God, regardless of what you say.

When God speaks to a person, revealing His plans and purpose, it will always cause a crisis of belief.

 As a review of Day 2 and Day 3 of this week, complete the first two statements about this crisis of belief.

1. An encounter with God requires _____.

2. Encounters with God are _____.

3. What you do in response to God's revelation (invitation) reveals what you believe about God.

4. True faith requires action.

In each of the last two statements circle one or two key words that might help you remember the points.

What you believe about God will determine what you do and how you live.

What you do reveals what you believe about God, regardless of what you say. When God reveals what He has purposed to do, you face a crisis—a decision time. Your response will reveal what you really believe about God.

David's Faith Demonstrated

 In the following paragraphs, underline what David believed about God based on what he said. I have underlined one for you.

David

In 1 Samuel 16:12-13 God told Samuel to anoint David to become the next king over Israel. In 1 Samuel 17 God brought David into the middle of His activity. Saul was still king of Israel, and the Israelites were at war with the Philistines. David was sent by his father to visit his older brothers in the army. When David arrived, Goliath (a giant soldier nine feet tall) challenged Israel to send one man to fight him. The losing nation would become the slaves of the winner (v. 9).

Israel's army was terrified. David asked in amazement, "Who is this uncircumcised Philistine that he should defy the armies of the <u>living God</u>?" (v. 26). David faced a crisis of belief. He may have realized that God had brought him to the battlefield and had prepared him for this assignment.

David said he would fight this giant. He stated his belief, "The Lord who delivered me from the paw of the lion and the paw of the bear will deliver me from the hand of this Philistine" (v. 37). David refused to take the normal weapons of war. Instead, he took a sling and five smooth stones. He said to Goliath, "You come against me with sword and spear and javelin, but I come against you in the name of the Lord Almighty, the God of the armies of Israel, whom you have defied. This day the Lord will hand you over to me . . . and the whole world will know that there is a God in Israel. All those gathered here will know that it is not by sword or spear that the Lord saves; for the battle is the Lord's, and he will give all of you into our hands" (vv. 45-47). David killed Goliath, and Israel went on to victory.

What did David say he believed about God?

_____

Based on David's response to Goliath, what do you think David believed about God?

_____

David's statements indicate he believed God was the living God and that He was Deliverer. David's actions verified he really did believe these things about God. Many thought David was a foolish young boy, and even Goliath laughed at him. God delivered the Israelites, however. He gave a mighty victory through David, so that the whole world would know there was a God in Israel!

Sarai's Lack of Faith

God called Abram and promised to make his offspring as numerous as the stars. Abram questioned God about this promise, since he remained childless into his old age. God reaffirmed, "'A son coming from your own body will be your heir' . . . . Abram believed the Lord, and he credited it to him as righteousness" (Gen. 15:4, 6).

Abram's wife, Sarai, was more than 70 years old at this time. Since she was past childbearing years, she decided she would have to "build a family" in a different way. She gave her maid to Abram as a wife, and Ishmael was born to Hagar a year later. Sarai's actions indicated what she believed about God.

 Which of the following more closely indicates what Sarai seemed to *believe* about God? Check your response.

❏ a. God could do anything—even give her a child of her own.

❏ b. God could not possibly give her a child of her own at age 77, and He needed her help in finding a way for Abram to become a father.

Do you see how Sarai's actions told what she really believed about God? She did not have the faith to believe God could do the impossible and give her a child at age 77. Her belief about God was limited by her own human reason. This act of unbelief was very costly. Ishmael caused Abram and Sarai much grief in their old age. Ishmael and his descendants have lived in hostility toward Isaac and the Jews from that time until today. What you *do* in response to God's invitation really does indicate what you believe about God.

 Read the following case studies. Evaluate the response of the individuals and churches to determine what they really believe about God. Check your response, or write your own conclusion to each situation.

1. After months of prayer and counseling with her youth pastor and her pastor, Sheri believed that God was calling her into full-time Christian service. To prepare for this ministry, she felt that she should pursue studies at a Christian university. In a talk with her older brother, he reminded her that their parents had always expected her to become a doctor, like her father. Her brother was persuasive. So, not wanting to disappoint her parents, Sheri decided not to pursue her sense of calling to mission service. What do you think Sheri believes about God?

   ❏ a. God will convince her parents that she is truly called.
   ❏ b. God has the right to direct her life as He pleases.
   ❏ c. God may have been able to part the Red Sea, but He could never change the minds of her parents.
   ❏ d. Other _____

2. Jon is shy but is a strong Christian in the eyes of his schoolmates. To his surprise, he was nominated for president of a Christian club in his school.

By his actions, David revealed what he believed about God.

Abram questioned God

Sarai

Unbelief is very costly.

Since Jon had never considered himself to be a leader, he responded to the nomination by saying, "I don't have the qualifications for the job." What do you think Jon believes about God?

❏ a. The Holy Spirit will enable me to do anything He wants me to do.

❏ b. God can't do anything through me that I am not able to do myself.

❏ c. Other _____

3. Teresa and Betsy were on a double-blind date. The two guys took them to a wild party. They knew they shouldn't be there, but they were afraid they would be the laughing stock of their school if they told their dates to take them home. After discussing the situation, they decided to smile and say nothing so they wouldn't appear prudish. What do you think they believe about God?

❏ a. God will give them the right words to say, so they might have a positive effect on their dates.

❏ b. God is strong enough to even convince their dates that what they are doing is wrong.

❏ d. Other _____

4. The youth group of Trinity Baptist Church felt led to conduct children's backyard Bible studies in a lower-income area in their city. The youth pastor estimated the cost of the project at $800. The budget and finance committees of the church turned down the project. The buck stopped there. The youth then decided not to pursue the ministry. What did this youth group believe about God?

❏ a. God leads us to agree to do many things but does not give us what we need to get the job done.

❏ b. God expects us to find ways to do a job that He leads us to pursue.

❏ c. A church can only do what it can afford.

❏ d. Other _____

When Sheri made her decision, she said more about her confidence in God than about her parents. Jon said more about his belief in God than about his abilities. When Teresa and Betsy decided to stay at the party, their actions did not match what they claimed to believe. The youth group at Trinity Baptist Church said far more about what they believe about God than what they believe about their resources.

Actions Speak

When God invites you to join Him and you face a crisis of belief, what you do next tells what you believe about God. Your actions really do speak louder than words.

 Read the following Scriptures and answer the questions.

Matthew 8:5-13. What did the centurion do to demonstrate his faith?

_____

What do you think the centurion believed about Jesus' authority and healing power?

_____

Matthew 8:23-27. What did the disciples do to demonstrate their "little faith" in the middle of this storm?

_____

Matthew 9:20-22. What did the woman do to demonstrate her faith?

_____

What do you think the woman believed about Jesus' power to heal?

_____

Matthew 9:27-31. What trait of God (Jesus) were these blind men appealing to? (v. 27).

_____

On what basis did Jesus heal these two men? (v. 29)

_____

Complete the third statement on the crisis of belief in your own words.

1. An encounter with God requires faith.

2. Encounters with God are God-sized.

3. What I do in response to God's revelation (invitation) reveals . . .

_____

4. True faith requires action.

When the blind men demonstrated that they believed Jesus was merciful and was the Messiah (Son of David), Jesus healed them according to their faith. The woman believed that just a touch of Jesus' garment would allow His healing power to flow to her. She was willing to risk public ridicule in order to experience His healing power. When the storms of life overtake us, we often respond as if God does not exist or does not care. Jesus rebuked the disciples for their failure to recognize His presence, protection, and power, not for their human tendency to fear. "Just say the word, and my servant will be healed," the centurion claimed. Jesus commended the centurion's faith in His authority and power. What each of these people did indicated to Jesus what kind of faith they had.

 Review today's lesson. Pray and ask God to identify one or more statements or Scriptures that He wants you to understand, learn, or practice. Underline it (them). Then respond to the following:

What was the most meaningful statement or Scripture you read today?

_____

Reword the statement or Scripture into a prayer of response to God.

_____

_____

What does God want you to do in response to today's study?

_____

Practice quoting your Scripture memory verses aloud or write them on separate paper.

SUMMARY STATEMENTS
- What I do reveals what I believe about God, regardless of what I say.
- What I believe about God will determine what I do and how I live.

DAY 5

TRUE FAITH REQUIRES ACTION

Faith without action is dead!

James emphasized, "As the body without the spirit is dead, so faith without deeds is dead" (Jas. 2:26). When you face a crisis of belief, what you do demonstrates what you believe. Faith without action is dead!

 Take a moment to review this unit by filling in the blanks in the following four statements.

1. An encounter with God requires _____.

2. Encounters with God are God-_____.

3. What I do in response to God's _____ (invitation) reveals what I _____ about God.

4. True faith requires _____.

Hebrews 11 is sometimes called "The Roll Call of Faith." Let's take a look at the actions of these individuals who demonstrated their faith.

 Turn to Hebrews 11. The following list on the left includes people commended for their faith in Hebrews 11. The verses of the chapter are in parentheses beside the name. Read the verses. Match the person on the left with the action on the right that demonstrated his or her faith. Write the correct letters in the blanks. Some of the names will have more than one letter.

_____ 1. Abel (v. 4)

_____ 2. Enoch (vv. 5-6)

_____ 3. Noah (v. 7)

_____ 4. Abraham (vv. 8-19)

_____ 5. Joseph (v. 22)

_____ 6. Moses (vv. 24-28)

_____ 7. Israelites (vv. 29-30)

_____ 8. Rahab (v. 31)

_____ 9. Jacob (v. 21)

A. Chose to be mistreated along with God's people
B. Offered a righteous sacrifice to God
C. Left Egypt
D. Made his home in a foreign country
E. Marched around the walls of Jericho
F. Pleased God by earnestly seeking Him
G. Blessed the sons of Joseph
H. Followed God without knowing where he was going
I. Kept the Passover
J. Passed through Red Sea on dry ground
K. Welcomed and hid the Israelite spies
L. Considered God faithful to keep His promises
M. Built an ark to save his family
N. Offered Isaac as a sacrifice
O. Gave instruction to bury his bones in Egypt

In the previous list of actions, circle the word (verb) in each lettered item that indicates an action taken as a demonstration of faith.

Based on Hebrews 11, is the following statement true or false? Check one.

Genuine faith is demonstrated by action. True ❑ False ❑

Answers are: 1-B; 2-F; 3-M; 4-DHLN; 5-O; 6-ACI; 7-EJ; 8-K; 9-G; and true.

While you are studying Hebrews 11, you may notice that a faithful life does not always bring the same results in human terms.

Read Hebrews 11:32-38. Based on your own evaluation, list the "good" outcomes of a faithful life on the left and the "bad" outcomes on the right. I have listed two to get you started.

"Good" Outcomes | "Bad" Outcomes

defeated enemies | *stoned to death*

Verses 33-35a describe the victory and deliverance some people of faith experienced. Verses 35b-38 describe the torture, mockery, and death other people of faith experienced. Were some more faithful than the others? No. "These were all commended for their faith" (Heb. 11:39). They decided a "Well done!" from their Master was more important than life itself. Hebrews 11:40 explains that God has planned something far better for people of faith than the world has to offer. Therefore:

> Since we are surrounded by such a great cloud of witnesses, let us throw off everything that hinders and the sin that so easily entangles, and let us run with perseverance the race marked out for us. Let us fix our eyes on Jesus, the author and perfecter of our faith, who for the joy set before him endured the cross, scorning its shame, and sat down at the right hand of the throne of God. Consider him who endured such opposition from sinful men, so that you will not grow weary and lose heart (Heb. 12:1-3).

Outward appearances of success do not always indicate the presence of faith, and outward appearances of failure do not always indicate lack of faith. A faithful servant is one who does what his Master tells him, whatever the outcome may be. Just like Jesus—He endured the cross. But now He is seated near the very throne of God! What a reward for faithfulness! Don't grow weary in being faithful. A reward is awaiting faithful servants.

 Write your Scripture memory verse for this unit.

_____

_____

_____

I pray that you are trying to please God by earnestly seeking Him (Heb. 11:6). In the next unit we will look more carefully at the cost factors in following God's will. Part of the action required to demonstrate your faith will be the adjustment you must make to God. Following God's will always requires adjustments that are costly to you and even to those around you.

Take time to review some of your responses at the end of each day in Units 1-6. Has God led you to do something that you did not do because you lacked faith? Yes ❑ No ❑ If yes, describe what you may need to do to demonstrate your faith in Him, His purposes, and His ways.

_____

_____

Spend some time praying about your faithfulness. Ask God to increase your faith.

Review today's lesson. Pray and ask God to identify one or more statements or Scriptures that He wants you to understand, learn, or practice. Underline it (them). Then respond to the following:

What was the most meaningful statement or Scripture you read today?

_____

Reword the statement or Scripture into a prayer of response to God.

_____

_____

What does God want you to do in response to today's study?

_____

_____

Review your Scripture memory verses and be prepared to recite them to a partner in your small-group session this week.

SUMMARY STATEMENTS

- Faith without action is dead!
- Genuine faith is demonstrated by action.
- God has planned something far better for people of faith.
- Don't grow weary in being faithful. A reward awaits faithful servants.

ADJUSTING YOUR LIFE TO GOD

THE PARTY GIRL

Kathryn was in the second grade when she began to realize she needed to have Jesus in her life. She and her mother met with her pastor to talk about her feelings. She vividly remembers accepting Christ in the pastor's study that day.

What Kathryn doesn't remember is when the joy of her salvation began to fade. It all happened so gradually. She took her first drink of alcohol when she was in junior high. Soon she was part of the "in" crowd and became popular. By the ninth grade, Kathryn was considered a "Party Girl."

Little by little, Kathryn started pulling away from the youth group at church. Then she started giving her mother a hard time about going to church at all. The whole family's attendance at church dwindled to almost nothing. More and more, Kathryn became part of the non-church going crowd.

Late one Friday night, some of Kathryn's friends carried her into her house. She was dead drunk. The next morning she and her mother had a long talk. Her mother informed her that they were going to begin attending church on a regular basis—starting the next day.

At first, Kathryn hated going to church again. Gradually, though, she looked forward to the events. Still, she didn't change her partying life-style; she just participated in both kinds of activities. Then, in the summer after tenth grade, something happened that wasn't gradual. God spoke to her in a very clear way, showing her that she had to make a choice about which life-style to follow.

When Kathryn talked to her youth pastor about her experience, he told her that she probably would lose some of her friends if she got serious about her faith. She wasn't sure she could give up her friends. He urged her to pray for more "want to." She said she would.

God granted Kathryn's request by putting a desire for change within her heart. The change didn't happen overnight; but, in time, Kathryn was transformed by the renewing of her mind (Rom. 12:1-2). She did lose some of her popularity at school, but she gained popularity and respect among the youth group at church.

Because Kathryn adjusted her life to God, what Satan meant for evil, God used for good.

Unit

8

Any of you who does not give up everything he has cannot be my disciple.

—LUKE 14:33

Verse to Memorize
This Week

DAY 1

ADJUSTMENTS ARE NECESSARY

You cannot stay where you are and go with God.

Many of us want God to speak to us and give us an assignment. However, we are not interested in making any major adjustments in our lives. Biblically, that is impossible. Every time God spoke to people in the Scriptures about something He wanted to do through them, major adjustments were necessary. They had to adjust their lives to God. Once the adjustments were made, God accomplished His purposes through those He called.

A Second Critical Turning Point

1. Crisis of Belief

Adjusting your life to God is the second critical turning point in your knowing and doing the will of God. The first turning point was the crisis of belief—you must believe God is who He says He is and that He will do what He says He will do. Making the adjustment of your life to God also is a turning point. If you choose to make the adjustment, you can go on to obedience. If you refuse to make the adjustment, you could miss what God has in store for your life.

2. Major Adjustments

 If you have faith at the crisis of belief, what else is required as a demonstration of that faith? Fill in the blank below.

Reality 5: God's invitation for you to work with Him always leads you to a crisis of belief that requires faith and _____.

Once you come to believe God, you demonstrate your faith by what you DO. Some action is required. This action is one of the major adjustments we will focus on in this unit. Your obedience also will be a part of the action required.

FAITH → ACTION
ACTION = ADJUSTMENTS + OBEDIENCE

 In you own words, summarize what you see stated in the preceding box.

_____

Adjustments to God

God's revelation is your invitation to adjust your life to Him.

When God speaks to you, revealing what He is about to do, that revelation is your invitation to adjust your life to Him. Once you have adjusted your life to Him, His purposes, and His ways, you are in a position to obey. Adjustments prepare you for obedience.

- **Noah** could not continue life as usual and build an ark (Gen. 6).
- **Abram** could not stay in Haran and father a nation in Canaan (Gen. 12:1-8).
- **Moses** could not stay on the back side of the desert herding sheep and stand before Pharaoh at the same time (Ex. 3).
- **David** had to leave his sheep to become king (1 Sam. 16:1-13).
- **Amos** had to leave the sycamore trees to preach in Israel (Amos 7:14-15).
- **Jonah** had to leave his home and overcome a major prejudice to preach in Nineveh (Jonah 1:1-2; 3:1-2; 4:1-11).
- **Peter, Andrew, James**, and **John** had to leave their fishing businesses to follow Jesus (Matt. 4:18-22).
- **Matthew** had to leave his tax collector's booth to follow Jesus (Matt. 9:9).
- **Saul** (later Paul) had to completely change direction in his life in order to be used of God to preach the gospel to the Gentiles (Acts 9:1-19).

Enormous changes and adjustments had to be made! Some had to leave family and country. Others had to drop prejudices and change priorities. Everything had to be yielded to God and the entire life adjusted to Him. When the necessary adjustments were made, God began to accomplish His purposes through them. Each one learned that adjusting one's life to God is well worth the cost.

 Read Luke 14:33. Have you come to a place in your life where you are willing to yield "everything" to Christ to follow Him? Yes ❑ No ❑

In the last unit you studied the fifth reality in the sequence of God's working through His people. In this unit we will look at the sixth reality. To review and preview, fill in the blanks in the realities below.

5. God's invitation for you to work with Him always leads you to a _____ of _____ that requires _____ and _____ .

6. You must make major _____ in your life to join God in what He is doing.

You may be thinking: "But God will not ask ME to make major adjustments." If you look to Scripture for your understanding of God, you will see that God certainly does require adjustments of His people. He even required major adjustments of His own Son: "You know the grace of our Lord Jesus Christ, that though he was rich, yet for your sakes he became poor, so that you through his poverty might become rich" (2 Cor. 8:9).

If you want to be a follower of Jesus, you will have to make major adjustments in your life. Until you are ready to make any adjustment necessary to obey what God has said, you will be of little use to God. Your greatest single difficulty in following God may come at the point of the adjustment.

Our tendency is to want to skip the adjustment and go from believing God to obedience. If you want to follow Him, you don't have that choice. God's ways are so different from yours (Isa. 55:9) that the only way to follow Him is to adjust your life to His ways.

 Elisha and the Rich Young Ruler were given invitations to join God. Read about them and answer the following questions.

1. What adjustment was required of each person?

Elisha (1 Kings 19:15-21): _____

Rich Young Ruler (Luke 18:18-27): _____

2. What was the response of each person?

Elisha: _____

Rich Young Ruler: _____

3. What is "eternal life" according to John 17:3?

_____

The rich ruler came to Jesus, seeking eternal life. Jesus knew the man could not love God completely and love his money at the same time (Matt. 6:24). So, Jesus asked the man to put away the thing that had become his god—his wealth. The young ruler's love of money made him an idol worshiper (Eph. 5:5). Because he refused to make the necessary adjustment, he missed out on experiencing eternal life.

Elisha's response was quite different from that of the Rich Young Ruler. He was willing to leave family and career (farming) to follow God's call. You have heard

Even Jesus had to make major adjustments.

Your greatest single difficulty in following God may come at the point of the adjustment.

"As the heavens are higher than the earth, so are my ways higher than your ways and my thoughts than your thoughts."

—Isaiah 55:9

"Now this is eternal life: that they may know you, the only true God, and Jesus Christ, whom you have sent."

—John 17:3

Rich Young Ruler

Elisha

the phrase about "burning your bridges behind you." Well, Elisha burned his farm equipment and killed his 24 oxen. He cooked the meat and fed the people of the community. He was not about to turn back! When he made the necessary adjustments, he was in a position to obey God. As a result, God worked through Elisha to perform some of the greatest signs and miracles recorded in the Old Testament (2 Kings 2—13). Elisha had to make the adjustments on the front end of his call. When he made the adjustments, God was able to work through him to accomplish the miracles.

> No one can sum up all God is able to accomplish through one solitary life, wholly yielded, adjusted, and obedient to Him!

 Do you want to be one who is wholly yielded, adjusted, and obedient to God? Yes ❑ No ❑

As you come to know and do the will of God, in what order do the following responses come? Number them in the correct order. (Refer to the seven realities on the inside back cover if you need help.)

____ obedience   ____ adjustments   ____ faith

When God invites you to join Him, the task will have such God-sized dimensions you will face a crisis of belief. Your response will first require faith. Faith will be demonstrated by action. The first action will involve the adjustment of your life to God. The second action will be your obedience to what God asks you to do. You cannot go on to obedience without first making the adjustments. So the sequence of responses is faith—adjustment—obedience.

 Review today's lesson. Pray and ask God to identify one or more statements or Scriptures that He wants you to understand, learn, or practice. Underline it (them). Then respond to the following:

What was the most meaningful statement or Scripture you read today?

_____

Reword the statement or Scripture into a prayer of response to God.

_____

What does God want you to do in response to today's study?

_____

Write your Scripture memory verse for this unit and review your other verses.

_____

SUMMARY STATEMENTS

- When God speaks to me, revealing what He is about to do, that revelation is my invitation to adjust my life to God.
- Adjustments prepare me for obedience.
- I cannot stay where I am and go with God.
- My greatest single difficulty in following God may come at the point of the adjustment.
- No one can sum up all God is able to accomplish through one solitary life, wholly yielded, adjusted, and obedient to Him!

KINDS OF ADJUSTMENTS

What kinds of adjustments of your life to God are required? Trying to answer that question is like trying to list all the things God might ask you to do. The list could be endless. I can, however, point you to some examples and give you some general categories of adjustments that may be required.

Adjustments may be required in one or more of the following areas:
- **In your circumstances** (like school activities, job, home, and others)
- **In your relationships** (friends, classmates, family, and others)
- **In your thinking** (prejudices, methods, your potential, and others)
- **In your commitments** (to family, church, school, plans, and others)
- **In your actions** (how you pray, give, serve, and others)
- **In your beliefs** (about God, your relationship to Him, and others)

The list could go on and on. The major adjustment will come at the point of acting on your faith. When you face the crisis of belief, you must decide what you believe about God. That mental decision may be the easy part. The hard part is adjusting your life to God and taking an action that *demonstrates* your faith. You may be called to attempt things that only *God* can do, where formerly you may have attempted only what you knew *you* could do.

 Read each of the following Scriptures. Determine the kind of adjustment that was (or is) required. Match the Scripture on the left with the correct adjustment required on the right. Some may call for more than one type of adjustment. Write a letter or letters in each blank.

Scriptures	Adjustments
_____ 1. Matthew 4:18-22	A. In circumstances
_____ 2. Matthew 5:43-48	B. In relationships
_____ 3. Matthew 6:5-8	C. In thinking
_____ 4. Matthew 20:20-28	D. In commitments
_____ 5. Acts 10:1-20	E. In actions
	F. In beliefs

Sometimes an adjustment may involve several of these areas at once. For instance, Peter's experience with Cornelius probably required adjustments in Peter's relationships with Gentiles, his commitments to the traditions of the Jews, and his actions regarding fellowship with Gentiles. The primary adjustments I see in the Scriptures above are: 1—A; 2—B or C; 3—E; 4—B, C, or E; 5—C or F. You may have seen others, and that is okay.

 List at least four areas in which God may ask you to make an adjustment of your life to Him. I have given you one.

1. *beliefs* _____

2. _____

3. _____

4. _____

Now go back and give one example for each area. For instance, an adjustment in circumstances may require that you make new friends.

Absolute Surrender

You may have heard a person say something like this: "Don't ever tell God something you will NOT do. That is what He will ask you to do." God is not looking for ways to make you "squirm." He does, however, want to be Lord of your life. Whenever you identify a place where you refuse to allow His lordship, that is a place where He will go to work. God may or may not require you to do that very thing you identified, but He will keep working until you are willing for Him to be Lord of all. Remember, because God loves you, His will is always best for you! Any adjustment God expects you to make is for your good.

God wants to be Lord of your life.

The adjusting is always to a Person. You adjust your life to God. You adjust your viewpoints to be like His viewpoints. You adjust your ways to be like His ways. After you make the necessary adjustments, He will tell you what to do next to obey Him. When you obey Him, you will experience Him doing through you something only God can do.

You adjust to a Person.

First: Adjust

Then: Obey

 Describe at least one adjustment you have had to make in your thinking as you have studied this course. (One person might respond: "I had to accept the fact that I cannot do anything of Kingdom value apart from God. Instead of doing things for God, I now am watching and praying to see what God wants to do through me.")

_____

Has God asked you to make a major adjustment to Him? Yes ❑ No ❑ If so, briefly describe the required adjustment and your response.

_____

Read the following statements made by godly persons. Under each statement describe the kind of adjustment this person had made or was willing to make. In the first quote, for example, one adjustment David Livingstone was willing to make was to live in poverty as a missionary (in Africa) rather than to have riches as a physician in his homeland.

David Livingstone (medical missionary to Africa)—"I am a missionary, heart and soul. God Himself had an only Son, and He was a missionary and a physician. A poor, poor imitation I am, or wish to be, but in this service I hope to live. In it I wish to die. I still prefer poverty and missions service to riches and ease. This is my choice."[1]

Adjustment(s) _____

Jim Elliot (missionary to Quichua Indians in South America)—"He is no fool who gives what he cannot keep to gain what he cannot lose."[2]

Adjustment(s) _____

Josephine Scaggs, (longtime missionary to Africa) summed up commitment to knowing and doing God's will with this verse: "That I may know him, and the power of his resurrection, and the fellowship of his sufferings, being made conformable unto his death" (Phil. 3:10, KJV).[3]

Adjustment(s) _____

Oswald J. Smith (missionary statesman of Canada)—"I want Thy plan, O God, for my life. May I be happy and contented whether in the homeland or on the foreign field; whether married or alone, in happiness or sorrow, health or sickness, prosperity or adversity—I want Thy plan, O God, for my life. I want it; oh, I want it!"[4]

Adjustment(s) _____

C. T. Studd (missionary to China, India, and Africa)—"If Jesus Christ be God and died for me, then no sacrifice is too great for me to give for Him."[5]

Adjustment(s) _____

Some adjustments these Christians made or were willing to make include:

- David Livingstone considered the work of a missionary to Africa as a high honor, not a sacrifice.
- Jim Elliot was willing to give up earthly things for his heavenly reward. He was killed by South American Indians as he sought to spread the gospel.
- Josephine Scaggs depended on God's enabling power to do His will.
- Oswald Smith so wanted God's plan for his life that he was willing to be content with any pleasure or difficulty.
- C. T. Studd was willing to make any sacrifice for Jesus' sake.

 Draw a star beside the quote that is the most meaningful to you. Then think about the level of commitment reflected in that quote. If you are willing to make a similar commitment to the lordship of Christ, spend time in prayer expressing your willingness to adjust your life to Him.

I have tried to help you understand that you cannot stay where you are and go with God in obedience to His will. Adjustments must come first. Then you can follow in obedience. In the remainder of this unit we are going to be looking at the second and third points below:

You cannot stay where you are and go with God!

OBEDIENCE REQUIRES ADJUSTMENTS

1. You cannot stay where you are and go with God at the same time.
2. Obedience is costly to you and to those around you.
3. Obedience requires total dependence on God to work through you.

When you are willing to surrender everything to the lordship of Christ, you, like Elisha, will find that the adjustments are well worth the reward of experiencing God. If you have not come to the place where you have surrendered *all* to His lordship, decide today to deny yourself, take up your cross, and follow Him (see Luke 9:23).

 Review today's lesson. Pray and ask God to identify one or more statements or Scriptures that He wants you to understand, learn, or practice. Underline it (them). Then respond to the following:

What was the most meaningful statement or Scripture you read today?

_____

Reword the statement or Scripture into a prayer of response to God.

_____

What does God want you to do in response to today's study?

_____

SUMMARY STATEMENTS

- God is interested in my absolute surrender to Him as Lord.
- I adjust to a Person.
- Adjustments are well worth the reward of experiencing God.
- The God who calls me is also the One who will enable me to do His will.

OBEDIENCE IS COSTLY, PART 1

Obedience is costly to you.

You cannot stay where you are and go with God. You cannot continue doing things your way and accomplish God's purposes in His ways. For you to DO the will of God, you must adjust your life to Him, His purposes, and His ways.

 In this unit we are looking at three statements about adjustments and obedience. On the lines provided, write each statement in your own words from your perspective. Use "I" and "me" instead of "you."

1. You cannot stay where you are and go with God at the same time.

_____

2. Obedience is costly to you and to those around you.

_____

3. Obedience requires total dependence on God to work through you.

_____

Willingness to pay the price

Look at the second statement: Obedience is costly to you and to those around you. You cannot know and do the will of God without paying the price of adjustment and obedience. Willingness to pay the price of following His will is one of the *major adjustments*. This also is a point where churches will not know and experience the fulfilling of God's purposes and will through them, because they are not willing to pay the price of obedience.

The Cost: An Adjustment in Our Program

Some people in our Vancouver association sensed God might be calling them to a place of ministry. They asked me to share with them how they could know and follow God's call. For two days we spread the word that anyone sensing a call to ministry could come to an informal meeting. Seventy-five people came to hear me share. They all sensed God was calling them to some form of ministry. They said, "We need some training."

Leaders needed training

Within two weeks the number grew to 120. We began to identify needs and list training possibilities and so forth. In a small group of churches, a training program for 120 who sense God's call is a giant-size task. When we started to talk about providing training for this group, someone asked, "But, Henry, what about all of the program plans we have made for the fall?" This person knew that we probably could not do our fall program and the training for these 120 people.

 In light of what you have been studying, how would you respond to that question? What would you tell the 120 people?

_____

_____

I could have responded to this group of 120 people in several ways. I could have reported the large response in our newsletter and just asked people to praise God for what He was doing. Then I could have told these 120 that we already had our program set for the next year. They would have to wait a year so we could get these training plans into our program calendar. I could have stayed with our full program plans and done a token amount of training to pacify the 120. I didn't do that. I explained: "If God has called these folks to ministry and they need training, we must adjust our plans and program to what God is doing." That's what we did. We adjusted our plans to join God in what He was doing.

We say that God is Lord and that He can interrupt us anytime He wants. We just don't expect Him to do it. We expect Him to affirm everything we are doing and never ask us to change anything we have planned. If we want God to go down the channels that we have already established and protect our own plans, we are in trouble. When God invites us to join Him, we will have to make some major adjustments. Those adjustments and obedience to God's direction will be costly.

 Read Acts 9:1-25 and describe the adjustment Saul had to make. Describe the cost He had to pay to follow Christ.

_____

_____

Does God ever ask a person to change his or her plans or directions in order to follow Him? Yes ❑ No ❑

Saul (later named Paul) had to make a total about-face in the direction of his life. He went from persecuting Christians to proclaiming that Jesus was the Christ. God will ask you to follow Him in ways that require adjustments in your plans and direction. For Paul the adjustment was costly. It even put his life at risk with the Jews. The adjustments you have to make will be costly as well.

Saul (Paul)

The Cost: Enduring Opposition

 Read the following paragraphs and underline some of the costs of obedience. I have underlined one for you.

Opposition to new churches

In Saskatoon our church sensed very clearly that God had called us to start new churches all across our province. Though we were convinced of the awesome spiritual darkness in Canada, some did not see it. Some actively opposed us at almost every mission church we started. In Regina, the capital of our province, a full page article appeared in the paper <u>condemning us</u> for daring to start a new church in this city of 150,000. In Deschambault, our pastor was met on the street and cursed by a witch doctor.

Some in our own conference felt we were foolish to attempt new mission churches when we were so small ourselves. We were told not to ask for help if we got into trouble with salary support for mission pastors or other staff workers. Those who had not been with us when God spoke to us saw our efforts as "presuming on God." I soon discovered that every step of faith could be interpreted as presumption by others.

Later, as mission churches grew and became self-supporting, our critics realized this work was indeed of God. Many of these former critics were encouraged to take these same steps of faith in starting new churches. God helped us remain faithful to Him, with a heart full of love toward others; but that was costly.

List some of the "costs" described above that we had to pay in starting new churches.

_____

_____

Read 2 Corinthians 11:23-33 and list some of the costs Paul had to pay for following and obeying Christ.

_____

_____

Sometimes obedience to God's will leads to opposition and misunderstanding. Because of his obedience, Paul suffered much for the cause of Christ. The list of beatings, imprisonments, and danger sound like more than one person could bear. Paul concluded one letter by saying, "I bear on my body the marks of Jesus" (Gal. 6:17). Paul had not had these experiences before he began to do the will of his Lord. Obedience was costly to him. Even so, Paul still could say:

> I want to know Christ and the power of his resurrection and the fellowship of sharing in his sufferings, becoming like him in his death, and so, somehow, to attain to the resurrection from the dead. Not that I have already obtained all this, or have already been made perfect, but I press on to take hold of that for which Christ Jesus took hold of me (Phil. 3:10-12).

The apostle Paul revealed the adjustments that he made to do the will of God when he said, "I have become all things to all men so that by all possible means I might save some" (1 Cor. 9:22).

 Have you ever had an experience where your adjustment or obedience to God was very costly? Yes ❑ No ❑ If so, briefly describe that experience and the cost you had to pay.

_____

David Livingstone   Remember David Livingstone, the famous Nineteenth Century missionary from Scotland? He gave his life making Christ known in Africa. Perhaps his words of commitment may inspire you to pay the cost of following Christ:

> Lord, send me anywhere, only go with me.
> Lay any burden on me, only sustain me.
> Sever any tie but the tie that binds me to Thyself.
> —David Livingstone

 Review today's lesson. Pray and ask God to identify one or more statements or Scriptures that He wants you to understand, learn, or practice. Underline it (them). Then respond to the following:

What was the most meaningful statement or Scripture you read today?

_____

Reword the statement or Scripture into a prayer of response to God.

_____

What does God want you to do in response to today's study?

_____

Practice quoting or writing your Scripture memory verses.

SUMMARY STATEMENTS

- Obedience is costly to me and those around me.
- I cannot know and do the will of God without paying the price of adjustment and obedience.
- I must adjust my plans and program to what God is doing.

OBEDIENCE IS COSTLY, PART 2

One of the most demanding adjustments related to doing the will of God is deciding to obey even when obedience will be very costly to those around you. Obedience is costly to you *and* to those around you.

 Answer the following questions. Read the Scripture passage if you do not know the answer already.

1. When Moses was obedient and told Pharaoh to let Israel go, what did it cost the Israelites? (Ex. 5:1-21)

_____

2. When Jesus obeyed and went to the cross, what was the cost to His mother as she stood there and watched Him die? (John 19:17-37)

_____

3. When Paul was obedient in preaching the gospel to the Gentiles at Thessalonica, what did it cost Jason? (Acts 17:1-9)

_____

When Moses obeyed God, the work of the Israelites was increased, and Israelite foremen were beaten. They paid a high cost for Moses to do God's will.

Moses and the Israelites

When the Lord Jesus did the will of the Father and died on the cross, His mother, Mary, had to suffer the agony of watching her Son be cruelly killed. Jesus' obedience put His mother through a heart-breaking experience. His obedience put fear and pain in the lives of every one of His disciples.

Jesus and Mary

When Paul followed God's will in preaching the gospel, others were led to respond to God's work in their own lives. Jason was arrested by a rioting mob and accused of treason because of his association with Paul. Frequently, Paul's obedience to God's will endangered the lives of those who were with Him.

Paul and Jason

You must not overlook this very real element in knowing and doing the will of God. God will reveal His plans and purposes to you, but your obedience will cost you and others around you. If, for instance, you surrender your life to missions, it may cost those around you (your family, your friends, your church).

 Fill in the blanks in the following statements.

1. You cannot _____ where you are and go with _____ at the same time.

2. Obedience is _____ to you and to those _____ you.

3. Obedience requires total dependence on God to work through you.

Check your answers on page 127.

Cost to My Family for Me to Do God's Will

When Marilynn and I committed ourselves to do mission work, one of the great costs we had to face was what it would cost our children for me to be gone so much. Our oldest was eight when we went to Saskatoon. I was gone from home much of the time during those years the children were growing up. Marilynn also had to pay a high price by rearing all five children with me gone so much.

We believed God would honor our obedience to Him. We believed the God who called us would show us how to rear our children. We came to believe that the Heavenly Father, who loves His servants, could take better care of our children than we ever could. We believed God would show us how to relate to our children

I could trust Him to care for my family.

in a way that would make up for the lost time with them. Now, I could not let that become an excuse for neglecting my family. But, when I was obeying the Father, I could trust Him to care for my family.

God took care of Marilynn.

I remember a time when Marilynn hit a low point. She had gotten discouraged. The next Sunday, after I preached, our son Richard came down the aisle to make a decision. He said, "I feel called to the ministry."

Right behind him came our neighbor, also named Richard. Marilynn had spent hundreds of hours taking care of this young lad from a troubled home. He came saying, "I also feel that God has called me to the ministry." Then he turned and said, "And a lot of the credit goes to Mom Blackaby."

Another boy named Ron stood up in that same service and said, "I want you to know that God is calling me to the ministry also. And I want you to know that it is due largely to Mother Blackaby." Marilynn had done much to show love to Ron. At this very critical time for Marilynn, God took care of her.

You can trust God with your family!

Now, all five of our children sense God's call to vocational ministry or mission work. Only God could have done such a beautiful work with our children. I want you to know that you can trust God with your family! I would rather entrust my family to God's care than to anyone else in the whole world.

 Have you made a commitment to Christ about your vocation that may require your family to pay a high price in the future? Yes ❑ No ❑ If so, briefly describe that decision or commitment.

_____

Can you recall a time when you chose not to obey God because of the potential high cost to those around you? Yes ❑ No ❑ If so, briefly describe the situation.

_____

What are some things you know about God that could help you trust God to care for you and those you love?

_____

Cost to an Individual for Our Church to Do God's Will

One of our new missions needed a building. The financial agency we were working with required that a certain percentage of the cost be paid as a down payment in order for us to get the loan. The mission was very small, so I asked our church members if they would be willing to pray about the possibility of contributing toward the down payment. They agreed to pray and watch to see how God would provide. Ivah Bates, one of our real prayers, was a widow. In addition to a small pension, she had a total of $4,000 in the bank to last her the rest of her life. She gave a check for $2,000 to the building fund.

"Don't deny my mother the right to give."

As Ivah's pastor, a whole lot of emotions went through my own heart. Here I was leading our church to do what we believed God wanted us to do. I had pain in my heart to see what it was costing our people to respond. I talked with Ivah's daughter. She said, "Don't deny my mother the right to give. She has always trusted her Lord. She wants to do that now, too."

Some pastors or finance committees say, "We can't ask our people to give too often, or it will hurt our ongoing budget giving." I learned to never deny God's people the opportunity to give. I never tried to pressure or manipulate people to give. That was not my job. I would create the opportunity and encourage them to give only what God led them to give. God's people will cheerfully do the will of God. Some of them will respond with generosity and count it an honor that God has allowed them to sacrifice for Him. Some will have life-changing experiences as a result of such an opportunity.

 Do you know of a situation where a person or a family had to pay a high price because your church followed God's will? Yes ❑ No ❑ If so, briefly describe the situation.

_____

_____

Complete the first two statements, then check your answers on page 131.

1. You cannot stay where you are and _____

2. Obedience is costly to _____

3. Obedience requires total dependence on God to work through you.

The Cry of a Mother's Heart

Hudson Taylor, a great man of prayer and faith, responded to God's call to go to China as a missionary. His father had already died; so he had to leave his widowed mother to go to China. By the end of his life in 1905, he had been used by God to found the China Inland Mission. There were 205 preaching stations, 849 missionaries, and 125,000 Chinese Christians—a testimony of a life absolutely surrendered to God. Hudson Taylor described something of the cost he and his mother experienced as he obeyed God's will to go to China as a missionary.

Hudson Taylor

 Imagine that you are Hudson Taylor. Your father is dead. You realize that you may never see your mother again here on earth. Slowly read Taylor's account of their parting and try to imagine the emotions they must have felt.

"My beloved, now sainted, mother had come to see me off from Liverpool. Never shall I forget that day, nor how she went with me into the little cabin [on the ship] that was to be my home for nearly six long months. With a mother's loving hand she smoothed the little bed. She sat by my side, and joined me in the last hymn that we should sing together before the long parting. We knelt down, and she prayed—the last mother's prayer I was to hear before starting for China. Then notice was given that we must separate, and we had to say good-bye, never expecting to meet on earth again.

"For my sake she restrained her feelings as much as possible. We parted; and she went on shore, giving me her blessing! I stood alone on deck, and she followed the ship as we moved towards the dock gates. As we passed through the gates, and the separation really commenced, I shall never forget the cry of anguish wrung from that mother's heart. It went through me like a knife. I never knew so fully, until then, what 'God so loved the world' meant. And I am quite sure that my precious mother learned more of the love of God to the perishing in that hour than in all her life before.

"Praise God, the number is increasing who are finding out the exceeding joys, the wondrous revelations of His mercies, vouchsafed to those who 'follow Him,' and emptying themselves, leave all in obedience to His great commission."[6]

Based on Taylor's brief account, answer the following questions:

1. What did it cost Hudson Taylor to adjust his life to God and obediently go to China?

_____

2. What did it cost Hudson's mother for him to obey God's will?

_____

3. What did they learn about God's love through this experience?

_____

Leaving home and family on a dangerous mission was a very costly step for Hudson Taylor to take. His mother so loved the Lord that she was willing to pay the cost of releasing her son to missions. Both of the Taylors had to pay a high cost for obedience. Yet, they both experienced the love of God in a way they had never known before.

 Do you think God might call you to a costly adventure of faith? Yes ❑ No ❑ How will you respond to God when He calls you to a costly commitment? Check one:

Yes, Lord! ❑ No, that costs too much. ❑

You may think the last question is a little premature. Not really. That is what the lordship of Christ is all about. You should be able to answer the last question without knowing anything about what God may call you to do. Your whole life should be lived with the attitude of "Lord, whatever you may ask of me today or in the future, my answer is YES!" Come to the place in your life where you are willing to surrender ALL to Him.

 Review today's lesson. Pray and ask God to identify one or more statements or Scriptures that He wants you to understand, learn, or practice. Underline it (them). Then respond to the following:

What was the most meaningful statement or Scripture you read today?

_____

Reword the statement or Scripture into a prayer of response to God.

_____

_____

What does God want you to do in response to today's study?

_____

SUMMARY STATEMENTS

- My obedience is costly to those around me.
- I can trust God to care for my family.
- Don't deny others the opportunity to sacrifice for their Lord.
- I need to trust Christ to communicate with His people.
- Lord, whatever you may ask of me today or in the future, my answer is yes!

TOTAL DEPENDENCE ON GOD

DAY 5

Obedience requires total
dependence on God to
work through you.

Another adjustment that is part of knowing and doing the will of God is coming to *a total dependence on God* to complete what He wants to do through you. Jesus said this relationship to Him would be like a vine and the branches: "Apart from me you can do nothing" (John 15:5). You must depend on God alone.

The adjustment requires moving from doing work *for* God according to *your* abilities, *your* gifts, *your* likes and dislikes, and *your* goals to being dependent on *God* and *His* working and *His* resources. This is a MAJOR adjustment!

 Fill in the blanks to complete the statements we have been studying in this unit.

1. You cannot _____ where you are and _____ with God at the same time.

2. Obedience is _____ to _____ and to those around you.

3. Obedience requires _____ _____ on God to work through you.

Check your answers on page 127.

Read the following Scriptures and notice why you must depend on God to carry out His purposes. Answer the question that follows.

> **John 15:5—**"I am the vine; you are the branches. If a man remains in me and I in him, he will bear much fruit; apart from me you can do nothing."

> **Galatians 2:20—**"I have been crucified with Christ and I no longer live, but Christ lives in me. The life I live in the body, I live by faith in the Son of God, who loved me and gave himself for me."

> **Isaiah 41:10—**"Do not fear, for I am with you; do not be dismayed, for I am your God. I will strengthen you and help you; I will uphold you with my righteous right hand."

> **Isaiah 46:9-11—**"I am God, and there is none like me . . . . My purpose will stand, and I will do all that I please . . . . What I have said, that will I bring about; what I have planned, that will I do."

Why must you depend totally on God to work through you?

_____

When God purposes to do something, He guarantees that it will happen. He is the One who will accomplish what He purposes to do. Without God at work in you, you can do nothing to bear Kingdom fruit. If you depend on anything other than God, you will be asking for failure in Kingdom terms.

The Bus Ministry Parable

Once a church asked, "God, how do you want to reach our community through us and build a great church?" God led them to start a bus ministry and provide transportation for children and adults to come to church. They did what God told them to do, and their church grew into a great church.

They were flattered when people from all over the country began to ask, "What are you doing to grow so rapidly?" They wrote a book on how to build great churches through a bus ministry. Thousands of churches bought buses to reach their communities. Later many sold the buses, saying, "It didn't work for us."

"IT" never does work!
HE works!

"IT" never works! HE works! The method is never the key to accomplishing God's purposes. The key is your relationship to a Person. When you want to know how God would have you reach your city or your schoolmates, start a new church or a backyard VBS group, or whatever, ask HIM.

 Answer the following questions by checking your responses.

1. Where do you usually go to find out how to accomplish God's purposes for your life or for your church? **Check all that apply.**
   - ❏ a. I go to a bookstore or library to find a book on the subject— written by a person who has a reputation for success in the area.
   - ❏ b. I talk to people or churches that are successful.
   - ❏ c. I talk to friends and ask them to tell me what decision to make.
   - ❏ d. I spend time in prayer and the Word asking God to guide me (us) to do things in His way.

2. Which of the following is most important for you to know in seeking to do God's will? Check one.
   - ❏ a. What God wants to do where I am
   - ❏ b. A successful method
   - ❏ c. What program will work best in my situation
   - o d. How other people or churches are succeeding in the Lord's work

Good books, successful methods, creative programs, and the success of others cannot take the place of your relationship with God. They never do the work. God does the work. Apart from Him, you can do nothing. By focusing on anything other than God as "the answer," you rob yourself of the joy of seeing God at work. You keep yourself from knowing God.

Only God has the right to tell you what to do.

Does that mean you will never be led by God to develop an organized program or follow a method? No. But only God has the right to tell you what to do. You do not take the initiative to decide for yourself what you will do. You must wait before God until He tells you what to do.

Wait on the Lord.

 Read the following Scriptures and circle the word *wait* in each verse.

Psalm 5:3—"In the morning, O Lord, you hear my voice; in the morning I lay my requests before you and wait in expectation."

Isaiah 40:31, KJV—"They that wait upon the Lord shall renew their strength; they shall mount up with wings as eagles; they shall run, and not be weary; and they shall walk, and not faint."

Why do you think you should wait until you have heard a word of direction from the Lord?

_____

"Ask and it will be given to you; seek and you will find; knock and the door will be opened to you. For everyone who asks receives; he who seeks finds; and to him who knocks, the door will be opened."

—Matthew 7:7-8

You may think of waiting as a inactive time. Waiting on the Lord is anything but inactive. While you wait on Him, you will be praying with a passion to know Him, His purposes, and His ways. You will be watching circumstances and asking God to interpret them by revealing to you His perspective. You will be sharing with other believers to find out what God is saying to them. As you wait on the Lord, you will be very active in asking, seeking, and knocking (Matt. 7:7-8). While you wait, continue doing the last thing God told you to do.

Then, when God gives you specific guidance, He will do through you more in days and weeks than you could ever accomplish in years of labor. Waiting on Him is always worth the wait. His timing and His ways are always right.

The Holy Spirit Helps You Accomplish the Father's Will

The Father has a purpose to work out through your life. In order that you not miss it, He places His Spirit in you. The Spirit's job is to guide you according to the will of the Father. He enables you to do God's will. You are completely dependent on God for the knowledge and ability to accomplish His purposes.

Jesus is your example of One who never failed to know and do the will of His Father. Everything the Father purposed to do through His life, the Lord Jesus did it immediately. What was the key to His success? He was always rightly related to the Father! In Jesus you have a picture of a solitary life in a love relationship with God, consistently living out that relationship. He is the perfect example. You and I will come quickly to the conclusion that we are a long way from that. True! But the Christ who lived His life in complete obedience is fully present in you to enable you to know and to do His will.

 How would you describe the quality and purity of your relationship with God?

_____

_____

_____

What, if any, adjustments do you think God wants you to make to renew a consistent and right relationship with Him?

_____

_____

Adjustments in Prayer and the Cost

When our church encountered a direction from God, I often experienced a crisis in my prayer life. The crisis was this: Was I willing to pray until God brought about His purposes? At such times, I learn more about prayer than almost any other time. Mark 11:24 is a prayer promise that has been challenging to me regarding the relationship of faith and prayer.

 Read Mark 11:24 (right) and write the promise in your own words.

_____

This verse is sometimes used to teach a "name-it-and-claim-it" theology. *You* decide what *you* want. *You* name that in *your* request, claim it, and it's *yours*. That is a self-centered theology. Remember that only God takes the initiative. He gives you the desire to do His will (Phil. 2:13). His Holy Spirit guides you to pray according to God's will (Rom. 8:26-28). The God-centered approach would be to let God lead you to pray according to His will (in the name and character of Jesus). Believe this: What God has led you to pray, He Himself will bring to pass. Then continue praying in faith and watching for it to happen.

When God encounters you, you face a crisis of belief that may require major adjustments in your life. You may need to spend much time in prayer. You may need to let God wake you up in the middle of the night to pray. Times may come when you pray into the night or even all night. Becoming a person of prayer requires a major adjustment of your life to God.

> "Whatever you ask for in prayer, believe that you have received it, and it will be yours."
>
> —Mark 11:24

Prayer is costly

Answer the following questions about your personal prayer life and the prayer life of your church.

1. Is your church known in your community as a "house of prayer"? Is your church a praying church? What evidence do you see that it is?

_____

2. What about your church youth group? Do members pray regularly? What can you do to help improve the prayer life of your youth group?

_____

3. What do you think God wants to do through you in regard to prayer in your church.

_____

> Every Christian needs
> to be a praying believer!
> Every church needs
> to be a praying church!

 Review today's lesson. Pray and ask God to identify one or more statements or Scriptures that He wants you to understand, learn, or practice. Underline it (them). Then respond to the following:

What was the most meaningful statement or Scripture you read today?

_____

Reword the statement or Scripture into a prayer of response to God.

_____

What does God want you to do in response to today's study?

_____

Review your Scripture memory verses and be prepared to recite them to a partner in your small-group session this week.

SUMMARY STATEMENTS

- Obedience requires total dependence on God to work through me.
- "IT" never works! HE works!
- The key is my relationship to a Person.
- Through me God will do more in days and weeks than I could ever accomplish in years of labor. Waiting on Him is always worth the wait.
- Fervent prayer will be one of the most demanding things I ever do.
- My church needs to be a praying church!
- I need to pray on a regular basis.

[1]David & Naomi Shibley, *The Smoke of a Thousand Villages*, (Nashville: Thomas Nelson Publishers, 1989), 11.

[2]Elisabeth Elliot, *Shadow of the Almighty. The Life and Testament of Jim Elliot* (New York: Harper & Brothers Publishers, 1958), 247.

[3]Chapel address, Southwestern Seminary, Fort Worth, Texas.

[4]Shibley, Thousand Villages,11.

[5]Shibley, Thousand Villages, 98.

[6]J. Hudson Taylor, *A Retrospect*, (Philadelphia: The China Inland Mission, n.d.), 39-40.

EXPERIENCING GOD THROUGH OBEDIENCE

OBEDIENCE PAYS

When Dale walked down the halls of Ferguson High everyone noticed him. He was absolutely good-looking! A big partier, he was everybody's friend. To top it all off, he was one half of the "Most Perfect Couple" at school. His girlfriend, Laura, was the captain of the cheerleading squad and had just been elected homecoming queen.

Dale had accepted Christ a year before he met Laura and was on a "spiritual" high for a while. However, when the beginning excitement subsided, so did his commitment. He seldom went to church these days.

Although Laura was a Christian and attended church regularly, her commitment to her Christian walk was not very deep. She did feel that it was important to be connected with church, and she persuaded Dale to attend church after they began to date. But she didn't want to get too "religious."

Dale's renewed involvement in church led him to be convicted about his life-style. At first, he chose to ignore God's voice. But, after several months, God's calling became too persistent to ignore. He went to see one of the youth counselors at church. That person explained to him that he needed to rededicate his life to Christ.

Although Dale fully understood that a recommitment to Christ might cost him some popularity, he firmly decided it was something he had to do. He was convinced God could do something better with his life than what he was doing. He did lose some of his popularity. And he even lost the "perfect" girlfriend. She told him she just couldn't handle a boyfriend that was *too Christian* (even though she brought him back to church in the first place). But, on the positive side, he lost the desire to go to the wild parties.

Dale has not looked back. Not even once has he regretted his decision to obey Christ completely. Through this obedience he has found a happiness and a walk with God that he didn't know existed.

> "No eye has seen, no ear has heard, no mind has conceived
> what God has prepared for those who love Him."
> —1 Corinthians 2:9

Unit

9

Jesus replied, "If anyone loves me, he will obey my teaching. My Father will love him, and we will come to him and make our home with him."

—John 14:23

*Verse to Memorize
This Week*

OBEDIENCE, PART 1

You come to know God by experience as you obey Him, and He accomplishes His work through you.

God has always been at work in our world. He is now at work where you are. God always takes the initiative to come to you and reveal what He is doing or what He is about to do. When He does, this will be His invitation for you to join Him.

Joining God requires major adjustments of your life to Him, so that He can accomplish His will through you. When you know what God has said, what He is about to do, and have adjusted your life to Him, there is yet one remaining necessary response to God.

> To experience God at work in and through you, you must obey Him. When you obey Him, He will accomplish His work through you; and you will come to know Him by experience.

This unit focuses on the last of our seven realities: You come to know God by experience as you obey Him, and He accomplishes His work through you.

 For review, see if you can write the seven realities in your own words, using the "hints" below.

1. Work _____

2. Love relationship _____

_____

3. Invitation _____

_____

4. Speaks _____

_____

5. Crisis _____

_____

6. Adjust _____

_____

7. Obey _____

_____

Check your answers on the inside back cover of the book.

Below, I have listed three actions from reality 7. Number them in the order that they occur as you follow God's will.

_____ a. You come to know God by experience.

_____ b. You obey Him.

_____ c. He accomplishes His work through you.

After God has taken the initiative to involve you in His work, you believe Him and adjust your life to Him. Only then do you get to the place of obedience. You must obey Him first. Then He will accomplish His work through you. When God does a God-sized work through your life, you come to know Him intimately by experience. The answer to the last question is a-3, b-1, c-2. In this unit you will study each of these aspects of God's work more fully.

You Obey Him

In Unit 4, Day 3 (pp. 60-62), you studied the relationship between love and obedience. You found that obedience is the outward expression of your love of God (John 14:15, 24a). Here are some statements from that lesson:
- Obedience is the outward expression of your love of God.
- The reward for obedience and love is that God will reveal Himself to you.
- If you have an obedience problem, you have a love problem.
- God is love. His will is always best.
- God is all knowing. His directions are always right.
- God is all powerful. He can enable you to do His will.
- If you love God, you will obey Him!

"*If you love me, you will obey what I command. . . . He who does not love me will not obey my teaching.*"
—*John 14:15, 24*

 If, in the last few weeks, one of the statements above has influenced the way you love and obey God, briefly describe what God has been doing regarding your love and obedience.

_____

_____

Your memory verse for this unit speaks of love and obedience. Begin memorizing it. Write it below.

_____

_____

Jesus said that the one who is in intimate relationship with Him ("brother," "sister," "mother") is the one who does the will of the Heavenly Father (Matt. 12:50). By obedience, a person indicates his or her love relationship with God (John 14:15-21).

James emphasized that faith which does not obey in actions has no life. When the disciples obeyed Jesus, they saw God's mighty power working in and around them. When they did not act in faith, they did not experience His mighty work.

In many ways, obedience is your moment of truth. What you DO will:

1. Reveal what you believe about God.
2. Determine whether you will experience His mighty work in you and through you.
3. Determine whether you will come to know God more intimately.

"Whoever does the will of my Father in heaven is my brother and sister and mother."
—Matthew 12:50

"Faith without works is dead."
—James 2:20, KJV

Moment of truth

 Read 1 John 2:3-6 below. Circle the word *know* each time it occurs. Underline *obey* and *obeys*. Draw a box enclosing the word *love*. Answer the questions that follow.

1 John 2:3-6: "We know that we have come to know him if we obey his commands. The man who says, 'I know him,' but does not do what he commands is a liar, and the truth is not in him. But if anyone obeys his word, God's love is truly made complete in him. This is how we know we are in him: Whoever claims to live in him must walk as Jesus did."

1. How can you know that you have come to know God in Jesus Christ?

_____

2. What is one clear indication that a person does not know Him?

_____

3. What does God do in the life of anyone who obeys His Word?

_____

As a review from Unit 4, fill in the blanks in the following statements with the correct words from the following list.

force   enable   right   true   best

4. Because God is love, His will is always _____.

5. Because God is all-knowing, His commands are always _____.

6. Because God is all-powerful, He can _____ me to do His will.

At a moment of truth when you must choose whether to obey God, you cannot obey Him unless you believe and trust Him. You cannot believe and trust Him unless you love Him. You cannot love Him unless you know Him.

Each "new" command of Jesus requires a new knowledge and understanding of Him. The Holy Spirit will teach you about Jesus, so you can trust Him and obey Him. Then you will experience Him in new ways. This is how you grow in Him. As 1 John 2:3-6 emphasizes: When you come to know Him, you will obey Him. If you do not obey Him, that indicates you do not know Him.

Jesus stated the truth a different way when He said, "Not everyone who says to me, 'Lord, Lord,' will enter the kingdom of heaven, but only he who does the will of my Father who is in heaven" (Matt. 7:21). Obedience is very important.

Answers to questions 4-6: 4-best, 5-right, 6-enable.

The Importance of Obedience

When God gives you a command, you are to obey it.

If you know God loves you, you should never question a command from Him. It will always be right and best. When He gives you a command, you are not just to observe it, discuss it, or debate it. You are to obey it.

 Remember Dale's experience told at the beginning of this unit? If faced with the same situation, how would you react? Check your response (be honest):

❑ 1. Just as Dale did. I would follow Christ without hesitation.
❑ 2. I would remain a "closet" Christian in order to keep *all* my friends.
❑ 3. Other: _____

List some of the benefits of obedience that are found in the following Scriptures.

> **Jeremiah 7:23:** "Obey me, and I will be your God and you will be my people. Walk in all the ways I command you, that it may go well with you."

Benefit of obedience: _____

> **Luke 6:46-49:** "Why do you call me, 'Lord, Lord,' and do not do what I say? I will show you what he is like who comes to me and hears my words and puts them into practice. He is like a man building a house, who dug down deep and laid the foundation on rock. When a flood came, the torrent struck that house but could not shake it, because it was well built. But the one who hears my words and does not put them into practice is like a man who built a house on the ground without a foundation. The moment the torrent struck that house, it collapsed and its destruction was complete."

Benefit of obedience: _____

John 7:16-17: "Jesus answered, 'My teaching is not my own. It comes from him who sent me. If anyone chooses to do God's will, he will find out whether my teaching comes from God.' "

Benefit of obedience: _____

God blesses those who are obedient to Him (Deut. 28:1-20). The benefits of obedience are beyond our imagination; but they include being God's people (Jer. 7:23), having a solid foundation when the storms of life come against you (Luke 6:46-49), and knowing spiritual truth (John 7:16-17).

Disobedience is a serious rejection of God's will. Deuteronomy 28:15-68 speaks of some of the costs of disobedience.

Disobedience is serious.

 How do you think God would describe your level of obedience?

_____

What (if anything) do you know God wants you to do that you are not doing?

_____

Consider this prayer for your own life:

> Teach me, O Lord, to follow your decrees;
>   then I will keep them to the end.
> Give me understanding, and I will keep your law
>   and obey it with all my heart.
> Direct me in the path of your commands,
>   for there I find delight.
> —Psalm 119:33-35

 Review today's lesson. Pray and ask God to identify one or more statements or Scriptures that He wants you to understand, learn, or practice. Underline it (them). Then respond to the following:

What was the most meaningful statement or Scripture you read today?

_____

Reword the statement or Scripture into a prayer of response to God.

_____

What does God want you to do in response to today's study?

_____

SUMMARY STATEMENTS

- I come to know God by experience as I obey Him and He accomplishes His work through me.
- If I love God, I will obey Him.
- Obedience is the outward expression of my love of God.
- Faith that does not obey in actions is dead.
- Obedience is my moment of truth.
- God blesses those who are obedient to Him.

DAY 2

Obedience means joy and uninterrupted fellowship with God.

OBEDIENCE, PART 2

What Is Obedience?

Many people today are so self-centered that they want to do their own "thing." They do not stop to consider what obedience may mean in their lives. Jesus told a parable about obedience:

> "What do you think? There was a man who had two sons. He went to the first and said, 'Son, go and work today in the vineyard.'
> " 'I will not,' he answered, but later he changed his mind and went. Then the father went to the other son and said the same thing. He answered, 'I will, sir,' but he did not go."
>
> —Matthew 21:28-30

 Which son did the will of his father? Circle one: First son   Second son

What is the meaning of obedience? Check one.

❏ 1. Saying you will do what is commanded.
❏ 2. Doing what is commanded.

At the end of each day's lesson, you have been asked this question: "What does God want you to do in response to today's study?" I want you to look back at your responses to that question for each lesson. Keep in mind that some of the things you listed may be long-term commitments. Pray before you begin this review and ask God to help you see your overall pattern of obedience or disobedience. Then review your responses to the last question at the end of each day. Mentally answer these two questions about each day's response:

1. Do I believe God clearly guided me to respond to the study that way?
2. Have I done all that God has asked me to do up to this time?

Do not proceed until you have completed your review.

Now, respond to the following. If you do not have an answer or response, go on to the next item.

A. What is one command or instruction you have obeyed?

_____

B. What is one long-term instruction you have only just begun to obey?

_____

C. What is one response that probably was YOUR idea and *not* God's command? **Explain your answer.**

_____

D. What is one command you have not obeyed?

_____

_____

E. Below is a scale from 0—Complete Disobedience to 10—Perfect Obedience (Only Jesus would qualify for a 10!). **Place an X to indicate how you think GOD would rate your life of obedience since you began studying this course.**

Complete   0—1—2—3—4—5—6—7—8—9—10   Perfect
Disobedience   Obedience

F. Why do you think He would rate you at that level?

_____

G. If there is a level of disobedience, what do you sense is the root cause?

_____

If this has not been a positive experience, don't despair. Let God use this time of evaluation to draw you back to Himself—into a relationship of loving obedience. God is interested in moving you from where you are to where He wants you to be in this love relationship. From that point you can experience all the joys that He has to offer.

Obey What You Already Know to Be God's Will

Some people want God to give them an assignment to do for Him. They vow that they will do whatever He asks. But when God observes their lives, He notices that they have not obeyed in the things He already has told them to do.

Do you think God would give new assignments to a servant who will not obey? ❏ Yes ❏ No ❏ I don't know

God gave Ten Commandments. Are you obeying them? Jesus has told you to love your enemies. Are you doing that? Jesus has told your church to make disciples of all nations. Are you doing all you know to obey Him? When God tells you, through Scripture, to live in unity with your Christian brothers and sisters, are you doing that?

God's commands are not given to you so you can pick and choose the ones you want to obey and forget about the rest. He wants you to obey *all* His commands out of your love relationship with Him. When He sees that you are faithful and obedient in a little, He will be able to trust you with more. The Holy Spirit will guide you daily to the specific commands God wants you to obey.

God's commands

Second Chances

Frequently, people ask me the question, "When people disobey God's will, does He give them a second chance?"

Read Jonah 1:1-17 and answer these questions:

Jonah

1. What did God ask Jonah to do? (v. 2) _____

2. How did Jonah respond? (v. 3) _____

3. Then how did God respond to Jonah? (vv. 4-17) _____

_____

Now read Jonah 2:9—3:10 and answer these questions:

4. When God gave Jonah a second chance, how did Jonah respond? (3:3)

_____

_____

5. When Jonah obeyed God, what did God do through Jonah's ministry? (3:4-10)

_____

_____

God often gives a second chance.

I am comforted to know that God often gives a second chance. When God had a plan to call Nineveh to repentance, He asked Jonah to join Him in His work. Jonah disobeyed because he was prejudiced against those "pagan enemies." Jonah went through the trauma of being thrown into a raging sea and spending three days in the belly of a big fish. Jonah confessed and repented of His disobedience. Then God gave him a second chance to obey.

Jonah preached a one-sentence message, and God used the message to call 120,000 people to repentance. Jonah said, "I knew that you are a gracious and compassionate God, slow to anger and abounding in love" (Jonah 4:2). God's response to Jonah and Nineveh taught Jonah much about how deeply God cares for all peoples and wants them to come to repentance.

God does not give up on you.

If God allowed people only one mistake, Moses would never have come to be the person he was. He made several mistakes (for example, Ex. 2:11-15). Abraham started out with a great walk of faith, but He went into Egypt and blew it—more than once (for example, Gen. 12:10-20). David muffed it (for example, 2 Sam. 11), and so did Peter (for example, Matt. 26:69-75). Saul (Paul) even began his "service for God" by persecuting Christians (see Acts 9:1-2).

Disobedience Is Costly

Disobedience, however, is never taken lightly by God. You read how Jonah's disobedience almost cost him his life. Moses' murder of the Egyptian cost him 40 years in the wilderness. David's sin with Bathsheba cost the life of his son. Paul's early ministry was hindered because of his disobedience. Many people were afraid to get near him because of his reputation as a persecutor of Christians.

God is interested in developing your character.

God is interested in developing your character. At times He lets you move in the wrong direction, but He will never let you go too far without using discipline to bring you back. He may let you make a wrong decision. Then the Spirit of God causes you to recognize that it is not God's will. He guides you back to the right path. He will even take the circumstance of your disobedience and work that together for good (Rom. 8:28) as He corrects you and teaches you His ways.

Moses stole God's glory

Even though God forgives and often gives second chances, you must not take disobedience lightly. Moses stole God's glory in front of all Israel and struck the rock saying, "Listen, you rebels, must we bring you water out of this rock?" (Num. 20:10). Notice the word "we." God was the One who would bring water from the rock. Moses took God's glory, and God refused to take away the consequences of that disobedience. He refused to allow Moses to go into the promised land.

Mark the following statements as T (true) or F (false).

_____ 1. God never gives second chances.

_____ 2. When God forgives the sin of disobedience, He also removes all the consequences of the sin.

_____ 3. God can take the circumstances of disobedience and work them together for good for those who love Him.

_____ 4. God is interested in developing your character.

_____ 5. Disobedience can be very costly.

_____ 6. God does not always remove the consequences of sin.

God loves you. He wants what is the very best for you. That is why He gives you the instructions He does. His commands are not to limit or restrict you but to free you to experience the most meaningful life possible. Answers to the true and false questions: 1 and 2 are false. The others are true.

Obedience means joy and fellowship with God. A hymn by John H. Sammis reminds us of the relationship between obedience and fellowship with God:

> When we walk with the Lord In the Light of His Word
>   What a glory He sheds on our way!
> While we do His good will, He abides with us still,
>   And with all who will trust and obey.
>
> But we never can prove The delights of His love
>   Until all on the altar we lay;
> For the favor He shows And the joy He bestows
>   Are for them who will trust and obey.
>
> Then in fellowship sweet We will sit at His feet
>   Or we'll walk by His side in the way;
> What He says we will do, Where He sends we will go;
>   Never fear, only trust and obey.
>
> *Trust and obey, for there's no other way*
>   *To be happy in Jesus, But to trust and obey.*

Trust and Obey

Affirmation

When God invites us to join Him, we often want a sign: "Lord, prove to me this is You, and then I will obey." When Moses stood before the burning bush and received his invitation to join God, God told him he would receive a sign that God would send him. God told Moses, "This will be the sign to you that it is I who have sent you: When you have brought the people out of Egypt, you will worship God on this mountain" (Ex. 3:12). God's sign was going to come *after* Moses obeyed. Most of the time, this is the case in Scripture. Affirmation comes after the obedience.

A sign for Moses

Affirmation comes after the obedience.

God is love. Trust Him and believe Him. Because you love Him, obey Him. Then you will so fellowship with Him that you will come to know Him intimately.

 Review today's lesson. Pray and ask God to identify one or more statements or Scriptures that He wants you to understand, learn, or practice. Underline it (them). Then respond to the following:

What was the most meaningful statement or Scripture you read today?

_____

Reword the statement or Scripture into a prayer of response to God.

_____

What does God want you to do in response to today's study?

_____

SUMMARY STATEMENTS
- Obedience is doing what is commanded.
- I should obey what I already know to be God's will.
- When I am faithful and obedient in a little, God will trust me with more.
- God often gives second chances.
- Sometimes God does not give a second chance.
- Disobedience is costly.
- God is interested in developing my character.
- Affirmation comes after the obedience.

GOD WORKS THROUGH YOU

You, too, will be blessed when God does a special, God-sized work through you.

When you obey God, He will accomplish through you what He has purposed to do. When God purposes to do something through you, the assignment will have God-sized dimensions. This is because God wants to reveal Himself to you and those around you. If you can do the work in your own strength, people will not come to know God. However, if God works through you to do what only He can do, you and those around you will come to know Him.

Today's lesson is related to your study in Unit 7. The God-sized dimensions of an assignment from God create the crisis of belief. You have to believe that God is who He says He is and that He can and will do what He says He will do. When you obey Him, you have to allow Him to do what He has said. He is the one who accomplishes the assignment, but He does it through you.

Read the following statements from Unit 7 and check the ones that have been especially meaningful to you.

❑ When God invites you to join Him in His work, He has a God-sized assignment for you.

❑ When God calls you to join Him in a God-sized task, faith is required.

❑ When you face a crisis of belief, what you do next reveals what you really believe about God.

❑ Faith is in a Person.

❑ Faith is confidence that what God has promised or said *will* happen.

❑ When God speaks, He always reveals what He is going to do.

❑ If you have faith in the God who called you, you will obey Him; and He will bring to pass what He has purposed to do.

❑ Obedience indicates your faith in God.

❑ With faith, you can proceed confidently to obey God; because you know He is going to bring to pass what He purposes.

Briefly describe one thing God has done to bring meaning to your life regarding God-sized tasks, faith, and/or obedience.

_____

Moses Obeyed and God Accomplished . . .

Moses obeyed

Only in the act of obedience did Moses begin to experience the full nature of God. What he began to know about God grew out of his obedience to God. In Moses' life we can see this pattern of God speaking, Moses obeying, and God accomplishing what He purposed to do.

Read the following Scriptures and answer the questions for each one.

Exodus 7:1-6

1. What was Moses commanded to do? (v. 2) _____

_____

2. What did God say He was going to do? (v. 4) _____

_____

3. What would happen when Moses obeyed, and God did what He said? (v. 5)

_____

_____

Exodus 8:16-19

4. What did God command Moses and Aaron to do? (v. 16)

_____

5. How did Moses and Aaron respond? (v. 17) _____

_____

6. Who turned the dust into gnats? Moses and Aaron ❏ or God ❏ (v. 19)

We see this pattern throughout Moses' life:
- God invited Moses to join Him in what He was doing to deliver Israel.
- God told Moses what he was to do.
- Moses obeyed.
- God accomplished what He purposed to do.
- Moses and those around him came to know God more clearly and intimately.

When the people stood between the Red Sea and the oncoming Egyptian army, God told Moses to hold his staff over the sea. Moses obeyed. God parted the sea, and the people crossed on dry ground (see Ex. 14:1-25). Then Miriam led the people in a hymn of praise describing their new understanding of God.

When the people had no water to drink, they complained to Moses. God told Moses to strike a rock with the staff. Moses obeyed, and God caused water to flow from the rock (Ex. 17:1-7). We see this pattern in Moses' life again and again.

The stages in this pattern of God's working through Moses are in the wrong order below. Number them in the correct order from 1 to 5.

____ a. Moses and those around him came to know God more clearly.
____ b. Moses obeyed.
____ c. God told Moses what he was to do.
____ d. God accomplished what He purposed to do.
____ e. God invited Moses to join Him in delivering Israel.

When Noah obeyed, God preserved his family and repopulated the earth. When Abraham obeyed, God gave him a son and built a nation. When David obeyed, God made him a king. When Elijah obeyed, God sent down fire and consumed a sacrifice. These people of faith came to know God by experience when they obeyed Him and He accomplished His work through them. The correct order of stages in the pattern of God's working with Moses is: e, c, b, d, a.

The Disciples Obeyed and God Accomplished . . .

Luke recorded a beautiful experience of Jesus' disciples that follows this same pattern. Jesus invited 70 (72, NIV) to join Him in the Father's work. They obeyed and experienced God doing through them something only God could do.

Read Luke 10:1-24 and answer the following questions.

1. What did Jesus command the 70 followers to do?

In verse 2? _____

In verses 5 and 7? _____

_____

In verse 8? _____

In verse 9? _____

A pattern of God's working

70 disciples sent out

2. What does verse 16 indicate about the relationship between servants and the Master? Between the 70 and Jesus?

_____

3. How do you think the 70 felt about their experience? (v. 17)

_____

4. What do you think the 70 came to know about God through this experience?

_____

The disciples were blessed.

These disciples were blessed! They had been chosen by God to be involved in His work. What they saw, heard, and came to know about God was something even prophets and kings wanted to experience and did not (Luke 10:23-24).

You can experience rejoicing.

You, too, will be blessed when God does a special, God-sized work through you. You will come to know Him in a way that will bring rejoicing to your life. When other people see you experiencing God that way, they are going to want to know how they, too, can experience God that way. Be prepared to point them to God.

 Has God done something recently through you that has caused you to rejoice? Yes ❑ No ❑ If so, briefly describe the experience.

_____

"Let him who boasts boast in the Lord"

—1 Corinthians 1:31

If you are obedient, God will work some wonderful things through you. You will need to be very careful that any testimony about what God has done only gives glory to Him. Pride may cause you to want to tell your experience because it makes you feel special. That will be a continuing tension. You will want to declare the wonderful deeds of the Lord, but you must avoid any sense of pride. Therefore, "Let him who boasts boast in the Lord" (1 Cor. 1:31).

 Review today's lesson. Pray and ask God to identify one or more statements or Scriptures that He wants you to understand, learn, or practice. Underline it (them). Then respond to the following:

What was the most meaningful statement or Scripture you read today?

_____

Reword the statement or Scripture into a prayer of response to God.

_____

What does God want you to do in response to today's study?

_____

Practice quoting or writing your Scripture memory verses.

SUMMARY STATEMENTS

- When I obey God, He will accomplish through me what He has purposed to do.
- God wants to reveal Himself to me and those around me.
- I will be blessed when God does a special, God-sized work through me.
- I need to be very careful that any testimony about what God has done only gives glory to Him.
- "Let him who boasts boast in the Lord" (1 Cor. 1:31).

YOU COME TO KNOW GOD

When God works through you to accomplish His purposes, you come to know God by experience. You also come to know God when He meets a need in your life. In Unit 4 you learned that, in Scripture, the names of God indicate how He has revealed Himself to humanity.

 As a review, turn to page 55 and read "Knowing God by Experience" and "Names of God."

How does God reveal Himself to us? How do we come to know God?

_____

God revealed His personal name to Moses: "I AM WHO I AM" (Ex. 3:14). Jesus expressed Himself to His disciples by saying:

The I AM'S of Jesus

"I am the bread of life" (John 6:35).
"I am the light of the world" (John 8:12).
"I am the gate" (John 10:9).
"I am the good shepherd" (John 10:11).
"I am the resurrection and the life" (John 11:25).
"I am the way and the truth and the life" (John 14:6).
"I am the true vine" (John 15:1).

Jesus obviously identified Himself with the I AM of the Old Testament. Knowing and experiencing Jesus in these ways requires that you "believe in Him" (have faith in Him). For instance, when He says to you, "I am the way," what you do next in your relationship with Him will determine if you come to experience Him as "the way" in your own life. When you believe Him, adjust your life to Him, and obey what He says next, you come to know and experience Him as "the WAY." This is true about everything God reveals to you day-by-day.

 Using the names, titles, and descriptions of God on page 157, list below some names by which you have come to know God by experience.

_____

_____

_____

Which name of God is most precious or meaningful to you at this point in your life? Give a reason for your answer.

_____

_____

Use the remainder of this day in a time of prayer and thanksgiving to God for what He has revealed to you about Himself. You may want to use the helps on pages 58-59 to guide you in this time of worship and adoration of the Lord.

After your time of prayer and worship, write a description of how you have come to know God by experience during this course of study.

_____

_____

_____

DAY 5

QUESTIONS, ANSWERS, AND INVENTORY

God will never give me an assignment that He will not enable me to complete.

For a little change of pace, let's look at some questions related to this unit that I am commonly asked. Perhaps these are questions you, too, have been asking. After we look at the questions, I am going to ask you to take a personal inventory to examine and evaluate your experience during this course.

Question 1: Why does God seem to be working so slowly in my life?

On the evening before His crucifixion, Jesus told His disciples, "I have much more to say to you, more than you can now bear. But when he, the Spirit of truth, comes, he will guide you into all truth." (John 16:12-13). Jesus had more to teach His disciples, but they were not ready to receive it. He knew, however, that the Holy Spirit would continue to guide them into truth on God's timetable.

You may be saying, "God, hurry up and make me spiritually mature."

And God is saying, "I'm moving as fast in your life as you will allow Me. When you are ready for your next lesson, I will bring a new truth into your life."

 Ask yourself these questions:

- Am I responding to all God already is leading me to do?
- Have I obeyed all that I already know to be His will?
- Do I really believe He loves me and will always do what is best?
- Am I willing to patiently wait on His timing and obey everything I know to do in the meantime?

Why do you think God sometimes works slowly in a person's life as He matures him or her?

_____

Allow God to take all the time He needs.

Would you be willing for God to take all the time He needs to prepare you for the assignments He may have purposed for your life? If so, write out a prayer of commitment to Him.

_____

_____

Question 2: Why doesn't God give me a big assignment?

God might say to you, "You are asking Me to involve you in My great movements, but I am trying to get you simply to understand how to believe Me. I can't give you that assignment yet." God has to lay some basic foundations in your life before He can prepare you for the larger tasks.

Have you ever said something like, "Lord, if You just give me a great assignment, I will serve You for all I am worth"?

God might respond, "I really want to. But, if I were to put you into that kind of assignment, you would not be able to handle it. You just are not ready."

Are you able?

Then you may argue, "Lord, I can handle it; just try me." Do you remember any of the disciples who thought they were able to handle a bigger assignment?

On the night before Jesus' crucifixion Peter said, "Lord, I am ready to go with you to prison and to death."

Jesus responded, "I tell you, Peter, before the rooster crows today, you will deny three times that you know me." (Luke 22:33-34). Is it possible that He also knows exactly what you would do? Trust Him. Do not insist that He give you something you think you are ready for. He will move you into every assignment that He knows you are ready for.

 How do you think you should respond when God has not given you the kind of assignment you want?

_____

As you obey God, He will prepare you for the assignment that is just right for you. Any assignment, however, that comes from God is important. Don't use human standards to measure the importance or value of an assignment.

Question 3: What is happening when I obey, and the "doors" close?

Suppose you sense the call of God to a task, or to a place, or to an assignment. You proceed to do it, and everything goes wrong. Often people will say, "Well, I guess that just was not God's will."

Be very careful how you interpret circumstances. Many times we jump to a conclusion too quickly. God is moving us in one direction to tell us what He is about to do. We immediately jump to our own conclusion about what He is doing, because our conclusion sounds so logical. We have a tendency to leave the relationship and take things into our own hands. Don't do that.

Most of the time when God gives you a direction, His call is not what He wants you to do for Him. He is telling you what He is about to do where you are. For instance, God told Paul that He was going to reach the Gentiles through him. God, not Paul, was going to reach the Gentiles. Paul started to go in one direction, and the Spirit stopped him (Acts 16:6-10). He started to go another direction. Again, the Spirit stopped him. What was the original plan of God? To reach the Gentiles. What was Paul's problem? He was trying to figure out what he ought to do, and the "door" of opportunity closed. Did the door close? No. God was trying to say, "Listen to me, Paul. Go and sit in Troas until I tell you where you are supposed to go."

In Troas Paul had the vision to go over to Macedonia and help them. What was happening? God's plan was to take the gospel to the west toward Greece and Rome. God was at work in Philippi and wanted Paul to join Him.

 What are some of the things you would do when faced with a circumstance that seemed to close the door on God's will.

_____

When things seem to go wrong after you take a step of obedience:
• Clarify what God said and identify what may have been your "additions" to what He said.
• Keep in place what God has said.
• Let Him work out the details in His timing.
• Do all you know to do.
• Wait on the Lord until He tells you what to do next.

> The God who initiates His work in a relationship with you is the One Himself who guarantees to complete it.

Trust Him.

Any assignment from God is an important assignment.

"Paul and his companions traveled throughout the region of Phrygia and Galatia, having been kept by the Holy Spirit from preaching the word in the province of Asia. When they came to the border of Mysia, they tried to enter Bithynia, but the Spirit of Jesus would not allow them to. So they passed by Mysia and went down to Troas. During the night Paul had a vision of a man of Macedonia standing and begging him, 'Come over to Macedonia and help us.' After Paul had seen the vision, we got ready at once to leave for Macedonia, concluding that God had called us to preach the gospel to them."

—Acts 16:6-10

When things seem to go wrong . . . *Clarify what God said.*

Question 4: How can I know whether the word I receive is from God, my own selfish desires, or Satan?

Some people go to a lot of trouble studying Satan's ways so they can recognize when something appears to be a deception of Satan. I don't do that. I have determined not to focus on Satan. He is defeated. The One who is guiding me is the Victor. The only way Satan can affect God's work through me is when I believe Satan and disbelieve God. Satan cannot ultimately stop what God purposes to do.

 When you are faced with a sense of direction, you may ask, "Is this God, me, or Satan." How can you know clearly a word from God?

_____

Jesus quoted the last word He had from the Father.

How should you approach spiritual warfare with Satan? Know the ways of God so thoroughly that, if something doesn't measure up to God's ways, turn away from it. That's what Jesus did in the temptations. In essence Jesus quietly said, "I understand what you are saying, Satan; but that is not the last word I had from God. The Scriptures say . . . ." (see Matt. 4:1-11). Jesus just kept doing the last thing God told Him to do until God Himself told Him what to do next.

Question 5: Does God Have One Plan for My Life for Eternity?

Does God plan your life for eternity and then turn you loose to work out His plan? We get in trouble when we try to get God to tell us if He wants us to be a Christian business person, a music director, an education director, a preacher, a teacher, or a missionary. God doesn't usually give you a one-time assignment and leave you there forever. Yes, you may be placed in one job at one place for a long time; but God's assignments come to you on a daily basis.

God's plan is for a relationship.

God calls you to a relationship in which you are willing to do and be anything He chooses. If you will respond to Him as Lord, He may lead you to do and be things you would never have dreamed of. If you don't follow Him as Lord, you may miss something God wants to do through you.

God will never give you an assignment that He will not, at the same time, enable you to complete. That is what a spiritual gift is—a supernatural empowering to accomplish the assignment God gives you. Don't focus on your talents, abilities, and interests in determining God's will. I have heard so many people say, "I would really like to do that; therefore, it must be God's will." That kind of response is self-centered. You need to become God-centered. When He is Lord, your response should be something like this:

> *Lord, I will do anything that your kingdom requires of me. Wherever You want me to be, I'll go. Whatever the circumstances, I'm willing to follow. If you want to meet a need through my life, I am your servant; and I will do whatever is required.*

 Suppose a friend says to you, "I think God may be calling me to the ministry, but I don't know whether I should be a pastor, missionary, or minister of education? I want to be very careful. I don't want to miss God's plan for my life! How can I know what to do next?"

How would you respond? List or outline what you would say.

_____

_____

Did you point your friend to God's plan as a relationship, not just a job description? Did you help him see his need to submit to Christ's lordship on a daily basis? Did you suggest that he seek advice from your pastor or youth minister? Did you offer to arrange such a meeting? I trust you would have been able to help him to a God-centered approach to knowing and doing God's will.

Your Spiritual Inventory

In this time together, my prayer has been that you would come to know God more intimately as you experienced Him at work in and through your life. Today, I want you to briefly review the past 9 units and identify what God has been doing in your life. Then, I want you to spend time with the Lord taking a spiritual inventory of your present walk with Him. I hope you have come to this time with a deep sense of God's presence and activity in your life. What God has begun in your life, He Himself will bring to perfect completion! (Phil. 1:6)

"He who began a good work in you will carry it on to completion until the day of Christ Jesus."
—Philippians 1:6

A. In your own words write the seven realities of experiencing God. Check your work with the statements inside the back cover.

1.

2.

3.

4.

5.

6.

7.

Review

B. Which reality has been most meaningful to you and why?

_____

C. Review your 9 memory verses. Which one has been most meaningful to you and why?

_____

D. Briefly review your end-of-the-day responses. Which statement or Scripture has God used to touch your life most deeply?

_____

E. How did God use that statement or Scripture in your life?

_____

F. Describe your most meaningful experience of God during this study.

_____

G. What name of God has become the most meaningful to you and how?

_____

Ask the Holy Spirit to guide you as you respond to the following.

Spiritual checkup

H. Which of the following best describes how you feel about your love relationship with God? Check one or more.

❏ 1. Grows sweeter every day   ❏ 5. Needs a tune-up

❏ 2. A roller coaster ride   ❏ 6. Cold

❏ 3. Bubbling over with joy   ❏ 7. Solid as a rock

❏ 4. Lukewarm   Other: _____

I. Which of the following best describes how you feel about your relationship with your church, the body of Christ? Check one or more.

❏ 1. Ready for a marathon
❏ 2. In training
❏ 3. Out of shape

❏ 4. In intensive care
❏ 5. Satisfactory condition
Other: _____

Tomorrow and beyond

J. What is your greatest spiritual challenge?

_____

K. What would be the most meaningful thing your study group could pray about for your spiritual growth and walk with the Lord?

_____

L. What do you sense God would have you do next to continue your training as a disciple of Jesus Christ?

_____

M. What, if any, specific assignment(s) do you sense God has called you to join Him in doing?

_____

Others

N. How are you praying for your youth group and your church and her relationship to Christ?

_____

O. What does God want you to do to help others in their walk with the Lord? Check any that you sense God leading you to do or fill in the blank.

❏ 1. Bear witness to what God has done and is doing in my life.
❏ 2. Help someone in my youth group to know and experience God this way.
❏ 3. Offer to lead a group study of *Experiencing God, Youth Edition*.
❏ 4. Encourage other youth to participate in a study of *Experiencing God*.
Other: _____

Pray, thanking God for what He has done and what He is doing . . .

- in your life
- in your family
- in your small group

- in your church
- in your denomination
- in the world

God has been so gracious to allow me to join Him as He has been working in your life. I thank God for the many wonderful things He has done in our day. Now . . .

I pray that out of his glorious riches he may strengthen you with power through his Spirit in your inner being, so that Christ may dwell in your hearts through faith. And I pray that you, being rooted and established in love, may have power, together with all the saints, to grasp how wide and long and high and deep is the love of Christ, and to know this love that surpasses knowledge—that you may be filled to the measure of all the fullness of God.

Now to him who is able to do immeasurably more than all we ask or imagine, according to his power that is at work within us, to him be glory in the church and in Christ Jesus throughout all generations, for ever and ever! Amen.

—Ephesians 3:16-21

The following are names, titles, and descriptions of God found in the New International Version of the Bible.

FATHER

a faithful God who does no wrong
a forgiving God
a fortress of salvation
a glorious crown
a jealous and avenging God
a Master in heaven
a refuge for his people
a refuge for the needy in his distress
a refuge for the oppressed
a refuge for the poor
a sanctuary
a shade from the heat
a shelter from the storm
a source of strength
a stronghold in times of trouble
an ever present help in trouble
architect and builder
commander of the Lord's army
Creator of heaven and earth
defender of widows
eternal King
Father
Father of compassion
Father of our spirits
Father of the heavenly lights
father to the fatherless
God
God Almighty
God and Father of our Lord Jesus Christ
God Most High
God my Maker
God my Rock
God my Savior
God my stronghold
God of Abraham, Isaac, and Jacob
God of all mankind
God of glory
God of grace
God of hope
God of love and peace
God of peace
God of retribution
God of the living

God of truth
God our Father
God our strength
God over all the kingdoms of the earth
God the Father
God who gives encouragement
God who relents from sending calamity
great and awesome God
great and powerful God
he who blots out your transgressions
he who forms the hearts of all
he who raised Christ from the dead
he who reveals his thoughts to man
he who is able to do immeasurably more than all we ask or imagine
he who is able to keep you from falling
Holy Father
Holy One among you
I AM
I AM WHO I AM
Judge of all the earth
King of glory
King of heaven
living and true God
Lord (Adonai)
Lord God Almighty
Lord is Peace
Lord (Jehovah)
Lord Most High
Lord my Banner
Lord my Rock
Lord of heaven and earth
Lord of kings
Lord our God
Lord our Maker
Lord our shield
Lord who heals you
Lord who is there
Lord who makes you holy
Lord will Provide
love
Maker of all things
Maker of heaven and earth
Most High
my Comforter in sorrow
my confidence
my helper
my hiding place

my hope
my light
my song
my strong deliverer
my support
One to be feared
only wise God
our dwelling place
our judge
our lawgiver
our leader
Our Redeemer
Righteous Father
righteous judge
Rock of our salvation
Shepherd
Sovereign Lord
the compassionate and gracious God
the Eternal God
the consuming fire
the exalted God
the faithful God
the gardener (husbandman)
the glorious Father
the Glory of Israel
the God who saves me
the God who sees me
the living Father
the Majestic Glory
the Majesty in heaven
the one who sustains me
the only God
the potter
the rock in whom I take refuge
the spring of living water
the strength of my heart
the true God
you who hear prayer
you who test the heart and mind
you who keep your covenant of love

JESUS

a banner for the peoples
Alpha and Omega
Ancient of Days
Anointed One
apostle and high priest
author and perfecter of our faith
author of life
author of their salvation

blessed and only Ruler
Branch of the Lord
bread of life
bridegroom
chief cornerstone
Chief Shepherd
Christ Jesus my Lord
Christ Jesus our hope
Christ of God
consolation of Israel
covenant for the people
crown of splendor
eternal life
Faithful and True
faithful and true witness
first to rise from the dead
firstborn over all creation
fragrant offering and sacrifice to
   God
friend of tax collectors and "sinners"
God of all the earth
God over all
God's Son
great high priest
great light
great shepherd of the sheep
guarantee of a better covenant
he who gives life to the world
he who searches hearts and minds
head of every man
head of the church
head over every power and authority
heir of all things
him who died and came to life
   again
him who loves us and has freed us
   from our sins
his one and only son
Holy and Righteous One
holy servant Jesus
hope of Israel
horn of salvation
image of the invisible God
Immanuel (God with us)
indescribable gift
Jesus
Jesus Christ
Jesus Christ our Lord
Jesus Christ our Savior
Jesus of Nazareth
judge of the living and the dead
KING OF KINGS
King of the ages
Lamb of God
light for revelation to the Gentiles
light of life
light of the world
Lord and Savior Jesus Christ
Lord of glory

LORD OF LORDS
Lord of peace
Lord of the harvest
Lord of the Sabbath
man accredited by God
man of sorrows
Master
Mediator of a new covenant
merciful and faithful high priest
messenger of the covenant
Messiah
morning star
my friend
my intercessor
one who makes men holy
one who speaks to the Father in our
   defense
one who will rule over the nations
our God and Savior Jesus Christ
our only Sovereign and Lord
our Passover lamb
our peace
Physician
Prince of Peace
ransom for all men
refiner and purifier
resurrection and the life
righteous Judge
righteous man
Righteous One
Rock eternal (rock of ages)
ruler of God's creation
ruler of the kings of the earth
Savior of the world
Shepherd and Overseer of your
   souls
Son of Man
Son of the Blessed One
Son of the living God
Son of the Most High God
source of eternal salvation
sure foundation
Teacher
the Amen
the atoning sacrifice for our sins
the Beginning and the End
the bright Morning Star
the exact representation of his
   being
the First and the Last
the gate (door)
the good shepherd
the Head
the life
the Living One
the living Stone
the Lord our righteousness
the man Jesus Christ
the most holy

the One and Only
the only God our Savior
the radiance of God's glory
the rising of the sun (Dayspring)
the stone the builders rejected
the testimony given in its proper
   time
the true light
the true vine
the truth
the way
the Word (logos)
true bread from heaven
wisdom from God
witness to the peoples
Wonderful Counselor
Word of God
Word of life
your life
your salvation

HOLY SPIRIT

a deposit (earnest)
another Counselor
breath of the Almighty
Holy One
Holy Spirit
Holy Spirit of God
seal
Spirit of Christ
Spirit of counsel and of power
spirit of faith
spirit of fire
Spirit of glory
Spirit of God
spirit of grace and supplication
Spirit of his Son
Spirit of holiness
Spirit of Jesus Christ
spirit of judgment
spirit of justice
Spirit of knowledge and of the fear
   of the Lord
Spirit of life
Spirit of our God
Spirit of sonship (adoption)
Spirit of the living God
Spirit of the Lord
Spirit of the Sovereign Lord
Spirit of truth
Spirit of wisdom and of under
   standing
Spirit of wisdom and revelation
the gift
the promised Holy Spirit
the same gift
Voice of the Almighty
Voice of the Lord

I, _____

covenant with my Experiencing God group to do the following:

1. Complete the study of the *Experiencing God, Youth Edition*, workbook each week before the group session.

2. Pray regularly for other group members.

3. Participate in all group sessions unless urgent circumstance beyond my control prevent my attendance. When unable to attend, I will make up the session at the earliest possible time with the group leader or group member assigned.

4. Participate openly and honestly in the group sessions.

5. Keep confidential any personal matters shared by others in the group.

6. Be patient with my Christian brothers and sisters and my church as God works in us all to make us what He wants us to be. I will trust God to convince others of His will. I will not try to manipulate or pressure others to do what I think is best. I will simply bear witness of what I sense God may be saying to us and watch to see how the Spirit uses that witness.

7. Pray at least weekly for my pastor, my youth group, and my church.

Other prayer concerns:

_____

_____

_____

Signed: _____ Date: _____

Experiencing God Group Members:

_____

_____

_____

CHRISTIAN GROWTH STUDY PLAN

Preparing Christians to Serve

Christian Growth Study Plan
127 Ninth Avenue, North, MSN 117
Nashville, TN 37234-0117
FAX: (615) 251-5067

In the **Christian Growth Study Plan (formerly Church Study Course),** this book *Experiencing God, Youth Edition* is a resource for course credit in the subject area "Ministry" of the Christian Growth category of diploma plans. To receive credit, read the book, complete the learning activities, show your work to your pastor, a staff member or church leader, then complete the following information. This page may be duplicated. Send the completed page to:

For information about the Christian Growth Study Plan, refer to the current Christian Growth Study Plan Catalog. Your church office may have a copy. If not, request a free copy from the Christian Growth Study Plan office (615/251-2525).

Experiencing God, Youth Edition
COURSE NUMBER: CG- 0085
PARTICIPANT INFORMATION

Social Security Number   Personal CGSP Number*   Date of Birth

Name (First, MI, Last)
☐Mr.   ☐Miss
☐Mrs.   ☐

Home Phone

Address (Street, Route, or P.O. Box)   City, State   Zip Code

CHURCH INFORMATION

Church Name

Address (Street, Route, or P.O. Box)   City, State   Zip Code

CHANGE REQUEST ONLY

☐Former Name

☐Former Address   City, State   Zip Code

☐Former Church   City, State   Zip Code

Signature of Pastor, Conference Leader, or Other Church Leader   Date

*New participants are requested but not required to give SS# and date of birth. Existing participants, please give CGSP# when using SS# for the first time. Thereafter, only one ID# is required. *Mail To:* Christian Growth Study Plan, 127 Ninth Ave., North, MSN 117, Nashville, TN 37234-0117. Fax: (615) 251-5067